Great Battles of World War Two

# Battle of Okinawa

Compiled by

Eldon Mcmillian

*Scribbles*

Year of Publication 2018


ISBN : 9789352979349

Book Published by

# Scribbles

*(An Imprint of Alpha Editions)*

email - alphaedis@gmail.com


Produced by: PediaPress GmbH
Limburg an der Lahn
Germany
http://pediapress.com/

# Contents

# Introduction

## Battle of Okinawa

<table>
<tr><td colspan="2" align="center">Battle of Okinawa</td></tr>
<tr><td colspan="2" align="center">Part of the Pacific Theater of World War II</td></tr>
<tr><td colspan="2" align="center"><br>US Marine from the 2nd Battalion, 1st Marines on Wana Ridge provides covering fire with his Thompson submachine gun, May 18, 1945.</td></tr>
<tr><td align="center">Date</td><td>April 1 – June 22, 1945</td></tr>
<tr><td align="center">Location</td><td>Okinawa, Ryukyu Islands, Japan<br>26°30′N 128°00′E[1] Coordinates: 26°30′N 128°00′E[1]</td></tr>
<tr><td align="center">Result</td><td>Allied victory</td></tr>
<tr><td align="center">Territorial changes</td><td>Okinawa occupied by the US until 1972</td></tr>
<tr><td colspan="2" align="center">Belligerents</td></tr>
<tr><td>Ground Forces:<br>  United States<br>Naval Support:<br>  United States<br>  United Kingdom<br>  Canada<br>  New Zealand<br>  Australia</td><td>• Japan</td></tr>
<tr><td colspan="2" align="center">Commanders and leaders</td></tr>
</table>

| | |
|---|---|
| Simon Bolivar Buckner, Jr. † <br> Claudius Miller Easley † <br> Roy Geiger <br> Joseph Stilwell <br> Chester W. Nimitz <br> Raymond A. Spruance <br> William Halsey, Jr. | Mitsuru Ushijima † <br> Isamu Chō † <br> Minoru Ōta † <br> Seiichi Itō † <br> Hiromichi Yahara (POW) |

## Units involved

| | |
|---|---|
| *Ground units*: <br> **Tenth Army** <br> • XXIV Corps <br>   • 7th Infantry Division <br>   • 27th Infantry Division <br>   • 77th Infantry Division <br>   • 96th Infantry Division <br> • III Amphibious Corps <br>   • 1st Marine Division <br>   • 2nd Marine Division <br>   • 6th Marine Division <br> *Naval units*: <br> **Fifth Fleet** <br> • Task Force 50 <br>   • Task Force 58 <br>   • Task Force 57 <br> • Joint Exp. Force | *Ground units*: <br> **Thirty-Second Army** <br> • 24th Infantry Division <br> • 28th Infantry Division <br> • 62nd Infantry Division <br> • 44th Mixed Brigade <br> • 45th Mixed Brigade <br> • 59th Mixed Brigade <br> • 60th Mixed Brigade <br> • 27th Tank Regiment <br> *Naval units*: <br> **2nd Fleet** <br> **Combined Fleet** |

## Strength

| | |
|---|---|
| 541,000 in Tenth Army <br> 183,000 combat troops[2] rising to c. 250,000[3] | 76,000 Japanese soldiers, <br> 20,000 Okinawan conscripts[4] |

## Casualties and losses

| American | Japanese |
|---|---|
| **Personnel:** <br> 14,009 dead[5] to 20,195 dead[6,7,8] <br> • 12,520 killed in action[9] <br> 38,000 wounded[10] to 55,162 wounded[11] <br> **Materiel:** <br> 12 destroyers sunk <br> 15 amphibious ships sunk <br> 9 other ships sunk <br> 386 ships damaged <br> 763[12]–768[13] aircraft <br> 225 tanks destroyed. | **Personnel:** <br> From 77,166 killed[14] to 110,000 killed (US estimate) <br> More than 7,000 captured <br> **Materiel:** <br> 1 battleship sunk <br> 1 light cruiser sunk <br> 5 destroyers sunk <br> 9 other warships sunk <br> 1,430 aircraft lost[15] <br> 27 tanks destroyed <br> 743–1,712 artillery pieces, anti-tank guns, and anti-aircraft guns[16] |

40,000–150,000 civilians killed out of some est.300,000

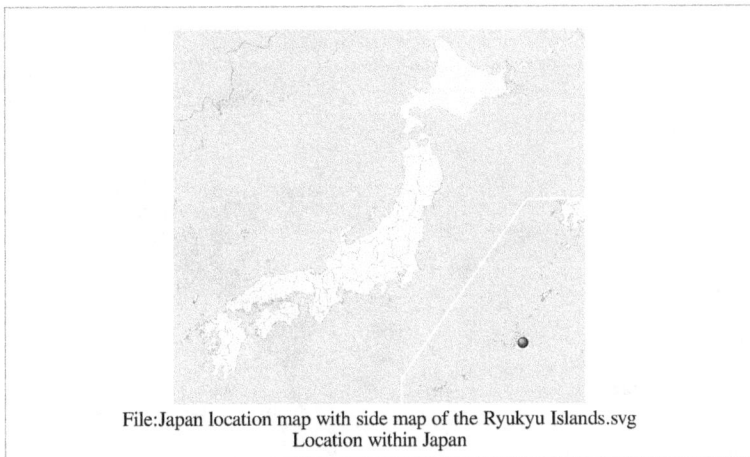
File:Japan location map with side map of the Ryukyu Islands.svg
Location within Japan

The **Battle of Okinawa** (Japanese: 沖縄□□ Hepburn: *Okinawa-sen*) (Okinawan: 沖縄□□ , translit. *Uchinaa ikusa*), codenamed **Operation Iceberg**, was a major battle of the Pacific War fought on the island of Okinawa by United States Marine and Army forces against the Imperial Japanese Army.[17] The initial invasion of Okinawa on April 1, 1945, was the largest amphibious assault in the Pacific Theater of World War II. The 82-day battle lasted from April 1 until June 22, 1945. After a long campaign of island hopping, the Allies were planning to use Kadena Air Base on the large island of Okinawa as a base for Operation Downfall, the planned invasion of the Japanese home islands, 340 mi (550 km) away.

The United States created the Tenth Army, a cross-branch force consisting of the 7th, 27th, 77th, and 96th infantry divisions of the US Army with the 1st, 2nd, and 6th divisions of the Marine Corps, to fight on the island. The Tenth was unique in that it had its own tactical air force (joint Army-Marine command), and was also supported by combined naval and amphibious forces.

The battle has been referred to as the "typhoon of steel" in English, and *tetsu no ame* ("rain of steel") or *tetsu no bōfū* ("violent wind of steel") in Japanese.[18] The nicknames refer to the ferocity of the fighting, the intensity of Japanese *kamikaze* attacks, and the sheer numbers of Allied ships and armored vehicles that assaulted the island. The battle was one of the bloodiest in the Pacific, with approximately 160,000 casualties on both sides: at least 75,000 Allied and 84,166–117,000 Japanese, including drafted Okinawans wearing Japanese uniforms. 149,425 Okinawans were killed, committed suicide or went missing, a significant proportion of the estimated pre-war 300,000 local population.

**Figure 1:** *A map of US operations at Okinawa*

In the naval operations surrounding the battle, both sides lost considerable numbers of ships and aircraft, including the Japanese battleship *Yamato*. After the battle, Okinawa provided a fleet anchorage, troop staging areas, and airfields in proximity to Japan in preparation for the planned invasion.

# Order of battle

## Allied

Central Pacific Task Forces (Fifth Fleet) under Admiral Raymond Spruance:

- Covering Forces and Special Groups (Task Force 50) directly under Spruance:
  - Fast Carrier Force (TF 58) under Vice Admiral Marc A. Mitscher with 88 ships (including 11 fleet carriers, 6 light carriers, 7 battleships and 18 cruisers);
  - British Carrier Force (TF 57) under Vice Admiral Sir Bernard Rawlings with 4 carriers, 2 battleships, 5 cruisers, 14 destroyers and fleet train;
- Joint Expeditionary Force (TF 51) under Vice Admiral Richmond K. Turner (who was holding position of Commander, Amphibious Forces, Pacific):
  - Amphibious Support Force (TF 52) under Rear Admiral William H. P. Blandy:

- TG 52.1: 18 escort carriers with 450 aircraft;
- Sl Escort Carrier Group: 4 escort carriers with Marine Aircraft Group 31 and 33;
- Mine Flotilla (TG 52.2)
- Underwater Demolition Flotilla (TG 52.11): 10 100-strong UDT aboard destroyer escorts
- 170 fire support landing craft
- Western Islands Attack Group (TG 51.1) under Rear Admiral Ingolf N. Kiland with 77th Infantry Division, 17 attack and attack cargo transporters, 56 LSTs and support vessels;
- Northern Attack Force (TF 53) under Rear Admiral Lawrence F. Reifsnider, Commander Amphibious Group 4, aboard USS *Panamint* (AGC-13) with III Amphibious Corps (Major General Roy Geiger) on 40+ attack and attack cargo transporters, 67 LSTs and support vessels;
- Southern Attack Force (TF 55) under Rear Admiral John L. Hall with XXIV Corps (Major General John R. Hodge);
- Demonstration Group (TG 51.2) with 2nd Marine Division (Major General Thomas E. Watson);
- Gunfire and Covering Support Group (TF 54) under Rear Admiral Morton L. Deyo with 10 old battleships, 11 cruisers and 30 destroyers.
- Expeditionary Troops (TF 56) under Lieutenant General Simon Bolivar Buckner, Jr. with 10th Army.

TF 56 was the largest force within TF 50 and was built around the 10th Army. The army had two corps under its command: the III Amphibious Corps, consisting of 1st and 6th Marine Divisions, and the XXIV Corps, consisting of the 7th and 96th Infantry Divisions. The 2nd Marine Division was an afloat reserve, and the 10th Army also controlled the 27th Infantry Division, earmarked as a garrison, and the 77th Infantry Divisions.

In all, the Army had over 102,000 soldiers (of these, 38,000+ were non-divisional artillery, combat support and HQ troops, with another 9,000 service troops), over 88,000 Marines and 18,000 Navy personnel (mostly Seabees and medical personnel). At the start of the Battle of Okinawa, the 10th Army had 182,821 personnel under its command. It was planned that General Buckner would report to Turner until the amphibious phase was completed, after which he would report directly to Spruance.

Although Allied land forces were entirely composed of American units, the British Pacific Fleet (BPF; known to the US Navy as Task Force 57) provided about ¼ of Allied naval air power (450 planes). It comprised a force which included 50 warships, of which 17 were aircraft carriers; while the British

**Figure 2:** *Japanese commanders of Okinawa (photographed early
in February 1945). In center: (1) Admiral Minoru Ota, (2) Lt.
Gen. Mitsuru Ushijima, (3) Lt. Gen. Isamu Cho, (4) Col. Hitoshi
Kanayama, (5) Col. Kikuji Hongo, and (6) Col. Hiromichi Yahara*

armored flight decks meant that fewer planes could be carried in a single aircraft
carrier, they were more resistant to *kamikaze* strikes.

Although all the aircraft carriers were provided by Britain, the carrier group
was a combined British Commonwealth fleet with, Australian, New Zealand
and Canadian, ships and personnel. Their mission was to neutralize Japanese
airfields in the Sakishima Islands and provide air cover against Japanese
*kamikaze* attacks. Most of the air-to-air fighters and the small dive bombers
and strike aircraft were US Navy carrier-based airplanes.

## Japanese

The Japanese land campaign (mainly defensive) was conducted by the 67,000-
strong (77,000 according to some sources) regular 32nd Army and some 9,000
Imperial Japanese Navy (IJN) troops at Oroku naval base (only a few hundred
of whom had been trained and equipped for ground combat), supported by
39,000 drafted local Ryukyuan people (including 24,000 hastily drafted rear
militia called *Boeitai* and 15,000 non-uniformed laborers). The Japanese had
used *kamikaze* tactics since the Battle of Leyte Gulf, but for the first time, they
became a major part of the defense. Between the American landing on April

1 and May 25, seven major *kamikaze* attacks were attempted, involving more than 1,500 planes.

The 32nd Army initially consisted of the 9th, 24th, and 62nd Divisions, and the 44th Independent Mixed Brigade. The 9th Division was moved to Taiwan before the invasion, resulting in shuffling of Japanese defensive plans. Primary resistance was to be led in the south by Lieutenant General Mitsuru Ushijima, his chief of staff, Lieutenant General Isamu Chō and his chief of operations, Colonel Hiromichi Yahara. Yahara advocated a defensive strategy, whilst Chō advocated an offensive one.

In the north, Colonel Takehido Udo was in command. The IJN troops were led by Rear Admiral Minoru Ōta. They expected the Americans to land 6–10 divisions against the Japanese garrison of two and a half divisions. The staff calculated that superior quality and numbers of weapons gave each US division five or six times the firepower of a Japanese division. To this, would be added the Americans' abundant naval and air firepower.

## Military use of children

In Okinawa island, middle school boys were organized into front-line-service Tekketsu Kinnōtai, while Himeyuri students were organized into a nursing unit.[19]

The Japanese Imperial Army mobilized 1,780 middle school boys aged 14–17 years into front-line-service. They were named "Tekketsu Kinnōtai" (ja:鉄血 勤皇隊 , Iron and Blood Imperial Corps). This mobilization was conducted by the ordinance of the Ministry of Army, not by law.

The ordinances mobilized the student as a volunteer soldier for form's sake. In reality, the military authorities ordered schools to force almost all students to "volunteer" as soldiers. Sometimes they counterfeited the necessary documents. About half of Tekketsu Kinnōtai were killed, including in suicide bomb attacks against tanks, and in guerrilla operations.

After losing the Battle of Okinawa, the Japanese government enacted new laws in preparation for the decisive battles in the main islands. These laws made it possible for boys aged 15 or older and girls aged 17 or older to be drafted into front-line-service.

**Figure 3:** *Tekketsu Kinnōtai child soldiers*

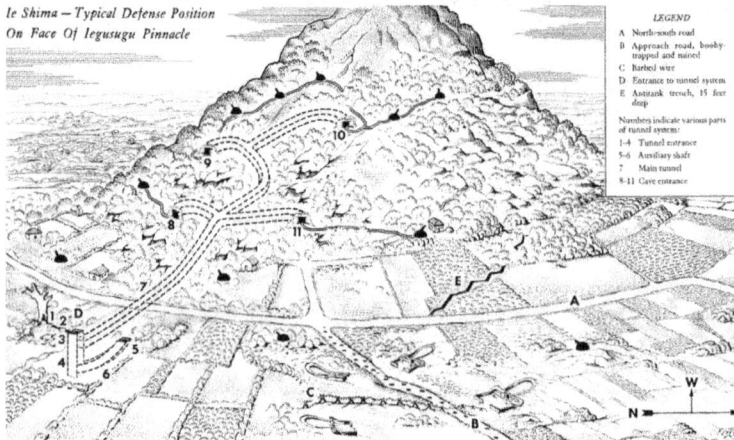

**Figure 4:** *A US military diagram of typical Japanese hill defensive tunnels and installations*

**Figure 5:** *A Japanese Type 89 150mm gun hidden inside a cave defensive system*

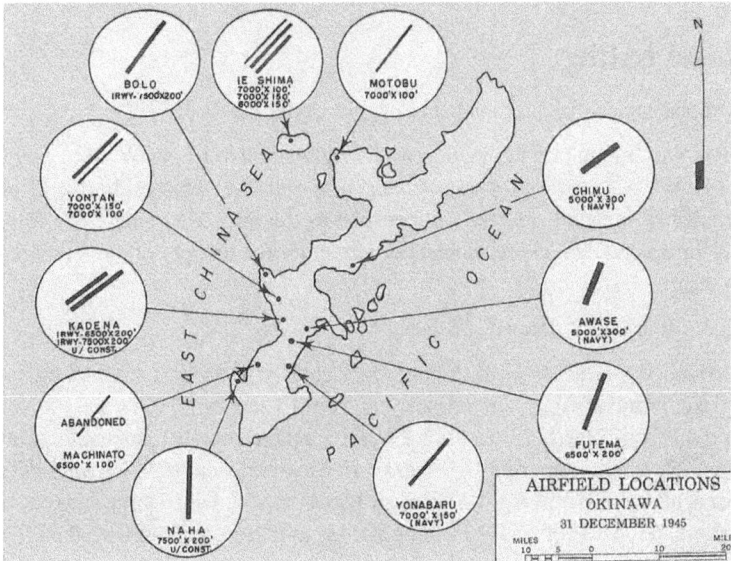

**Figure 6:** *A map of Okinawa's airfields, 1945*

**Figure 7:** *American aircraft carrier USS Bunker Hill burns after being hit by two kamikaze planes within 30 seconds.*

# Naval battle

<templatestyles src="Template:Quote_box/styles.css" />

There was a hypnotic fascination to the sight so alien to our Western philosophy. We watched each plunging *kamikaze* with the detached horror of one witnessing a terrible spectacle rather than as the intended victim. We forgot self for the moment as we groped hopelessly for the thought of that other man up there.

Vice Admiral C.R. Brown, US Navy[20]

The United States Navy's Task Force 58, deployed to the east of Okinawa with a picket group of from 6 to 8 destroyers, kept 13 carriers (7 CVs and 6 CVLs) on duty from March 23 to April 27 and a smaller number thereafter. Until April 27, a minimum of 14 and up to 18 escort carriers (CVEs) were in the area at all times. Until April 20, British Task Force 57, with 4 large and 6 escort carriers, remained off the Sakishima Islands to protect the southern flank.

The protracted length of the campaign under stressful conditions forced Admiral Chester W. Nimitz to take the unprecedented step of relieving the principal

**Figure 8:** *Royal Navy Fleet Air Arm Avengers, Seafires and Fireflies on HMS Implacable warm up their engines before taking off.*

naval commanders to rest and recuperate. Following the practice of changing the fleet designation with the change of commanders, US naval forces began the campaign as the US 5th Fleet under Admiral Raymond Spruance, but ended it as the 3rd Fleet under Admiral William Halsey.

Japanese air opposition had been relatively light during the first few days after the landings. However, on April 6, the expected air reaction began with an attack by 400 planes from Kyushu. Periodic heavy air attacks continued through April. During the period March 26 – April 30, twenty American ships were sunk and 157 damaged by enemy action. For their part, by April 30, the Japanese had lost more than 1,100 planes to Allied naval forces alone.

Between April 6 and June 22, the Japanese flew 1,465 *kamikaze* aircraft in large-scale attacks from Kyushu, 185 individual *kamikaze* sorties from Kyushu, and 250 individual *kamikaze* sorties from Formosa. While US intelligence estimated there were 89 planes on Formosa, the Japanese actually had about 700, dismantled or well camouflaged and dispersed into scattered villages and towns; the US Fifth Air Force disputed Navy claims of *kamikaze* coming from Formosa.[21]Wikipedia:Please clarify

The ships lost were smaller vessels, particularly the destroyers of the radar pickets, as well as destroyer escorts and landing ships. While no major Allied

**Figure 9:** *The super battleship Yamato explodes after persistent attacks from US aircraft.*

warships were lost, several fleet carriers were severely damaged. Land-based Shin'yō-class suicide motorboats were also used in the Japanese suicide attacks, although Ushijima had disbanded the majority of the suicide boat battalions prior to the battle due to expected low effectiveness against a superior enemy. The boat crews were re-formed into three additional infantry battalions.[22]

## Operation *Ten-Go*

Operation *Ten-Go* (*Ten-gō sakusen*) was the attempted attack by a strike force of 10 Japanese surface vessels, led by the *Yamato* and commanded by Admiral Seiichi Itō. This small task force had been ordered to fight through enemy naval forces, then beach *Yamato* and fight from shore, using her guns as coastal artillery and her crew as naval infantry. The *Ten-Go* force was spotted by submarines shortly after it left the Japanese home waters, and was intercepted by US carrier aircraft.

Under attack from more than 300 aircraft over a two-hour span, the world's largest battleship sank on April 7, 1945, after a one-sided battle, long before she could reach Okinawa. (US torpedo bombers were instructed to aim for only one side to prevent effective counter flooding by the battleship's crew, and to

**Figure 10:** *HMS Formidable on fire after a kamikaze at-tack on May 4. The ship was out of action for fifty minutes.*

aim for the bow or the stern, where armor was believed to be the thinnest.) Of *Yamato*'s screening force, the light cruiser *Yahagi* and 4 of the 8 destroyers were also sunk. The Imperial Japanese Navy lost some 3,700 sailors, including Admiral Itō, at the cost of 10 US aircraft and 12 airmen.

## British Pacific Fleet

The British Pacific Fleet, taking part as Task Force 57, was assigned the task of neutralizing the Japanese airfields in the Sakishima Islands, which it did successfully from March 26 to April 10.

On April 10, its attention was shifted to airfields on northern Formosa. The force withdrew to San Pedro Bay on April 23.

On May 1, the British Pacific Fleet returned to action, subduing the airfields as before, this time with naval bombardment as well as aircraft. Several *kamikaze* attacks caused significant damage, but since the British had armored flight decks on their aircraft carriers, they experienced only a brief interruption to their force's operations.

**Figure 11:** *The battleship USS Idaho shells Okinawa on April 1, 1945.*

# Land battle

The land battle took place over about 81 days beginning on April 1, 1945. The first Americans ashore were soldiers of the 77th Infantry Division, who landed in the Kerama Islands, 15 mi (24 km) west of Okinawa on March 26. Subsidiary landings followed, and the Kerama group was secured over the next five days. In these preliminary operations, the 77th Infantry Division suffered 27 dead and 81 wounded, while Japanese dead and captured numbered over 650. The operation provided a protected anchorage for the fleet and eliminated the threat from suicide boats.

On March 31, Marines of the Fleet Marine Force Amphibious Reconnaissance Battalion landed without opposition on Keise Shima, four islets just 8 mi (13 km) west of the Okinawan capital of Naha. A group of 155 mm (6.1 in) "Long Tom" artillery pieces went ashore on the islets to cover operations on Okinawa.

## Northern Okinawa

The main landing was made by the XXIV Corps and the III Amphibious Corps on the Hagushi beaches on the western coast of Okinawa on L-Day, April 1, which was both Easter Sunday and April Fools' Day in 1945. The 2nd

**Figure 12:** *US Marine reinforcements wade ashore
to support the beachhead on Okinawa, April 1, 1945.*

Marine Division conducted a demonstration off the Minatoga beaches on the southeastern coast to deceive the Japanese about American intentions and delay movement of reserves from there.

The 10th Army swept across the south-central part of the island with relative ease by World War II standards, capturing the Kadena and the Yomitan airbases within hours of the landing. In light of the weak opposition, General Buckner decided to proceed immediately with Phase II of his plan—the seizure of northern Okinawa. The 6th Marine Division headed up the Ishikawa Isthmus and by April 7, had sealed off the Motobu Peninsula.

Six days later on April 13, the 2nd Battalion, 22nd Marine Regiment, reached Hedo Point (Hedo-misaki) at the northernmost tip of the island. By this point, the bulk of the Japanese forces in the north (codenamed *Udo Force*) were cornered on the Motobu Peninsula. Here, the terrain was mountainous and wooded, with the Japanese defenses concentrated on Yae-Dake, a twisted mass of rocky ridges and ravines on the center of the peninsula. There was heavy fighting before the Marines finally cleared Yae-Dake on April 18. However, this was not the end of ground combat in northern Okinawa. On May 24, the Japanese mounted "Operation *Gi-gou*": a company of *Giretsu Kuteitai* commandos were airlifted in a suicide attack on Yomitan. They destroyed

**Figure 13:** *US Marines pass a dead Japanese*
*soldier in a destroyed village, April 1945.*

70,000 gallons of fuel and nine planes before being killed by the defenders, who lost two men.

Meanwhile, the 77th Infantry Division assaulted Ie Island (Ie Shima)—a small island off the western end of the peninsula—on April 16. In addition to conventional hazards, the 77th Infantry Division encountered *kamikaze* attacks, and even local women armed with spears. There was heavy fighting before the area was declared secured on April 21, and became another air base for operations against Japan.

## Southern Okinawa

While the 6th Marine Division cleared northern Okinawa, the US Army 96th and 7th Infantry Divisions wheeled south across the narrow waist of Okinawa. The 96th Infantry Division began to encounter fierce resistance in west-central Okinawa from Japanese troops holding fortified positions east of Highway No. 1 and about 5 mi (8 km) northwest of Shuri, from what came to be known as Cactus Ridge. The 7th Infantry Division encountered similarly fierce Japanese opposition from a rocky pinnacle located about 1,000 yd (910 m) southwest of Arakachi (later dubbed "The Pinnacle"). By the night of April 8, American troops had cleared these and several other strongly fortified positions. They

**Figure 14:** *A 6th Marine Division demolition crew watches explosive charges detonate and destroy a Japanese cave, May 1945.*

**Figure 15:** *American soldiers of the 77th Infantry Division listen impassively to radio reports of Victory in Europe Day on May 8, 1945.*

suffered over 1,500 battle casualties in the process, while killing or capturing about 4,500 Japanese. Yet the battle had only begun, for it was now realized that "these were merely outposts," guarding the Shuri Line.

The next American objective was Kakazu Ridge, two hills with a connecting saddle that formed part of Shuri's outer defenses. The Japanese had prepared their positions well and fought tenaciously. The Japanese soldiers hid in fortified caves. American forces often lost personnel before clearing the Japanese out from each cave or other hiding place. The Japanese sent Okinawans at gunpoint out to obtain water and supplies for them, which led to civilian casualties. The American advance was inexorable, but resulted in a high number of casualties on both sides.

As the American assault against Kakazu Ridge stalled, Lieutenant General Ushijima — influenced by General Chō — decided to take the offensive. On the evening of April 12, the 32nd Army attacked American positions across the entire front. The Japanese attack was heavy, sustained, and well organized. After fierce close combat, the attackers retreated, only to repeat their offensive the following night. A final assault on April 14 was again repulsed. The effort led the 32nd Army's staff to conclude that the Americans were vulnerable to night infiltration tactics, but that their superior firepower made any offensive Japanese troop concentrations extremely dangerous, and they reverted to their defensive strategy.

The 27th Infantry Division—which had landed on April 9—took over on the right, along the west coast of Okinawa. General John R. Hodge now had three divisions in the line, with the 96th in the middle, and the 7th to the east, with each division holding a front of only about 1.5 mi (2.4 km). Hodge launched a new offensive of April 19 with a barrage of 324 guns, the largest ever in the Pacific Ocean Theater. Battleships, cruisers, and destroyers joined the bombardment, which was followed by 650 Navy and Marine planes attacking the enemy positions with napalm, rockets, bombs, and machine guns. The Japanese defenses were sited on reverse slopes, where the defenders waited out the artillery barrage and aerial attack in relative safety, emerging from the caves to rain mortar rounds and grenades upon the Americans advancing up the forward slope.

A tank assault to achieve breakthrough by outflanking Kakazu Ridge failed to link up with its infantry support attempting to cross the ridge, and therefore failed with the loss of 22 tanks. Although flame tanks cleared many cave defenses, there was no breakthrough, and the XXIV Corps suffered 720 casualties. The losses might have been greater except for the fact that the Japanese had practically all of their infantry reserves tied up farther south, held there by another feint off the Minatoga beaches by the 2nd Marine Division that coincided with the attack.

**Figure 16:** *Lt. Col. Richard P. Ross Jr., commander of 3rd Battalion, 1st Marines braves sniper fire to place the United States' colors over the parapets of Shuri Castle on May 30. This flag was first raised over Cape Gloucester and then Peleliu.*

At the end of April, after Army forces had pushed through the Machinato defensive line,[23] the 1st Marine Division relieved the 27th Infantry Division, and the 77th Infantry Division relieved the 96th. When the 6th Marine Division arrived, the III Amphibious Corps took over the right flank and the 10th Army assumed control of the battle.

On May 4, the 32nd Army launched another counteroffensive. This time, Ushijima attempted to make amphibious assaults on the coasts behind American lines. To support his offensive, the Japanese artillery moved into the open. By doing so, they were able to fire 13,000 rounds in support, but effective American counter-battery fire destroyed dozens of Japanese artillery pieces. The attack failed.

Buckner launched another American attack on May 11. Ten days of fierce fighting followed. On May 13, troops of the 96th Infantry Division and 763rd Tank Battalion captured Conical Hill. Rising 476 ft (145 m) above the Yonabaru coastal plain, this feature was the eastern anchor of the main Japanese defenses and was defended by about 1,000 Japanese. Meanwhile, on the opposite coast, the 1st and 6th Marine Divisions fought for "Sugar Loaf Hill". The capture of these two key positions exposed the Japanese around Shuri on both

**Figure 17:** *A Japanese prisoner of war sits behind barbed wire after he and 306 others were captured within the last 24 hours of the battle by 6th Marine Division.*

sides. Buckner hoped to envelop Shuri and trap the main Japanese defending force.

By the end of May, monsoon rains which had turned contested hills and roads into a morass exacerbated both the tactical and medical situations. The ground advance began to resemble a World War I battlefield, as troops became mired in mud, and flooded roads greatly inhibited evacuation of wounded to the rear. Troops lived on a field sodden by rain, part garbage dump and part graveyard. Unburied Japanese and American bodies decayed, sank in the mud, and became part of a noxious stew. Anyone sliding down the greasy slopes could easily find their pockets full of maggots at the end of the journey.[24]

On May 29, Major General Pedro del Valle, commander of the 1st Marine Division, ordered Captain Julian D. Dusenbury of Company A, 1st Battalion, 5th Marines, to capture Shuri Castle. Seizure of the castle represented both strategic and psychological blows for the Japanese and was a milestone in the campaign. Del Valle was awarded a Distinguished Service Medal for his leadership in the fight and the subsequent occupation and reorganization of Okinawa. Captain Dusenbury would later receive the Navy Cross for his actions.

Shuri Castle had been shelled by the battleship USS *Mississippi* for three days before this advance. Due to this, the 32nd Army withdrew to the south and thus the Marines had an easy task of securing Shuri Castle. The castle, however, was outside the 1st Marine Division's assigned zone and only frantic efforts by the commander and staff of the 77th Infantry Division prevented an American air strike and artillery bombardment which would have resulted in many casualties due to friendly fire.

The Japanese retreat, although harassed by artillery fire, was conducted with great skill at night and aided by the monsoon storms. The 32nd Army was able to move nearly 30,000 personnel into its last defense line on the Kiyan Peninsula, which ultimately led to the greatest slaughter on Okinawa in the latter stages of the battle, including the deaths of thousands of civilians. In addition, there were 9,000 IJN troops supported by 1,100 militia, with approximately 4,000 holed up at the underground headquarters on the hillside overlooking the Okinawa Naval Base in the Oroku Peninsula, east of the airfield.

On June 4, elements of the 6th Marine Division launched an amphibious assault on the peninsula. The 4,000 Japanese sailors, including Admiral Minoru Ōta, all committed suicide within the hand-built tunnels of the underground naval headquarters on June 13. By June 17, the remnants of Ushijima's shattered 32nd Army were pushed into a small pocket in the far south of the island to the southeast of Itoman.

On June 18, General Buckner was killed by Japanese artillery fire while monitoring the progress of his troops from a forward observation post. Buckner was replaced by Roy Geiger. Upon assuming command, Geiger became the only US Marine to command a numbered army of the US Army in combat; he was relieved five days later by Joseph Stilwell. On June 19, General Claudius Miller Easley, the commander of the US Army's 96th Infantry Division, was killed by Japanese machine gun fire, also while checking on the progress of his troops at the front.

The last remnants of Japanese resistance ended on June 21, although some Japanese continued hiding, including the future governor of Okinawa Prefecture, Masahide Ōta. Ushijima and Chō committed suicide by *seppuku* in their command headquarters on Hill 89 in the closing hours of the battle. Colonel Yahara had asked Ushijima for permission to commit suicide, but the general refused his request, saying: "If you die there will be no one left who knows the truth about the battle of Okinawa. Bear the temporary shame but endure it. This is an order from your army Commander."[25] Yahara was the most senior officer to have survived the battle on the island, and he later authored a book titled *The Battle for Okinawa*. On August 15, 1945, Admiral Matome Ugaki was killed while part of a kamikaze raid on Iheyajima island. The official surrender ceremony was held on September 7, near Kadena airfield.

**Figure 18:** *Two US Coast Guardsmen pay homage to their comrade killed in the Ryukyu Islands.*

# Casualties

Okinawa was the bloodiest battle of the Pacific War. The most complete tally of deaths during the battle is at the Cornerstone of Peace monument at the Okinawa Prefecture Peace Park, which identifies the names of each individual who died at Okinawa in World War II. As of 2010, the monument lists 240,931 names, including 149,193 Okinawan civilians, 77,166 Imperial Japanese soldiers, 14,009 American soldiers, and smaller numbers of people from South Korea (365), the United Kingdom (82), North Korea (82) and Taiwan (34).

The numbers correspond to recorded deaths during the Battle of Okinawa from the time of the American landings in the Kerama Islands on March 26, 1945, to the signing of the Japanese surrender on September 2, 1945, in addition to all Okinawan casualties in the Pacific War in the fifteen years from the Manchurian Incident, along with those who died in Okinawa from war-related events in the year before the battle and the year after the surrender. 234,183 names were inscribed by the time of unveiling and new names are added each year. Forty thousand of the Okinawan civilians killed had been drafted or impressed by the Japanese army and are often counted as combat deaths.

**Figure 19:** *Two US M4 Sherman tanks knocked out by Japanese artillery at Bloody Ridge, April 20, 1945*

## Military losses

### American

The Americans suffered over 82,000 casualties, including non-battle casualties (psychiatric, injuries, illnesses), of whom over 12,500 were killed or missing. Battle deaths were 4,907 Navy, 4,675 Army, and 2,938 Marine Corps person-nel.[9] Several thousand personnel who died indirectly (from wounds and other causes) at a later date are not included in the total.

The most famous American casualty was Lieutenant General Simon Bolivar Buckner Jr., whose decision to attack the Japanese defenses head-on, although extremely costly in American lives, was ultimately successful. Four days from the closing of the campaign, Buckner was killed by Japanese artillery fire, which blew lethal slivers of coral into his body, while inspecting his troops at the front line. He was the highest-ranking US officer to be killed by en-emy fire during the Second World War. The day after Buckner was killed, Brigadier General Claudius Miller Easley was killed by Japanese machine gun fire. The famous war correspondent Ernie Pyle was also killed by Japanese machine gun fire on Ie Island (Ie Shima, a small island just off of northwestern Okinawa).[26]

Aircraft losses over the three-month period were 768 US planes, including those bombing the Kyushu airfields launching *kamikaze*s. Combat losses were 458, and the other 310 were operational accidents. On land, at least 225 tanks and many LVTs were lost. At sea, 368 Allied ships—including 120 amphibious craft—were damaged while another 36—including 15 amphibious ships and 12 destroyers—were sunk during the Okinawa campaign. The US Navy's dead exceeded its wounded, with 4,907 killed and 4,874 wounded, primarily from *kamikaze* attacks.

American personnel casualties included thousands of cases of mental breakdown. According to the account of the battle presented in *Marine Corps Gazette*:

> *More mental health issues arose from the Battle of Okinawa than any other battle in the Pacific during World War II. The constant bombardment from artillery and mortars coupled with the high casualty rates led to a great deal of personnel coming down with combat fatigue. Additionally the rains caused mud that prevented tanks from moving and tracks from pulling out the dead, forcing Marines (who pride themselves on burying their dead in a proper and honorable manner) to leave their comrades where they lay. This, coupled with thousands of bodies both friend and foe littering the entire island, created a scent you could nearly taste. Morale was dangerously low by the month of May and the state of discipline on a moral basis had a new low barometer for acceptable behavior. The ruthless atrocities by the Japanese throughout the war had already brought on an altered behavior (deemed so by traditional standards) by many Americans resulting in the desecration of Japanese remains, but the Japanese tactic of using the Okinawan people as human shields brought about a new aspect of terror and torment to the psychological capacity of the Americans.*

Medal of Honor recipients from Okinawa are:

- Beauford T. Anderson – April 13
- Richard E. Bush – April 16
- Robert Eugene Bush – May 2
- Henry A. Courtney Jr. – May 14–15
- Clarence B. Craft – May 31
- James L. Day – May 14–17
- Desmond Doss – April 29–May 21

### Japanese losses

The US military estimates that 110,071 Japanese soldiers were killed during the battle. This total includes conscripted Okinawan civilians.

A total of 7,401 Japanese regulars and 3,400 Okinawan conscripts surrendered or were captured during the battle. Additional Japanese and renegade Okinawans were captured or surrendered over the next few months, bringing the total to 16,346. This was the first battle in the Pacific War in which thousands of Japanese soldiers surrendered or were captured. Many of the prisoners were

**Figure 20:** *The last picture of US Army Lt. Gen. Simon Bolivar Buckner, Jr. (right), taken on June 18, 1945. Later in the day, he was killed by Japanese artillery fire.*

native Okinawans who had been pressed into service shortly before the battle, and were less imbued with the Imperial Japanese Army's no-surrender doctrine. When the American forces occupied the island, many Japanese soldiers put on Okinawan clothing to avoid capture, and some Okinawans would come to the Americans' aid by offering to identify these mainland Japanese.

The Japanese lost 16 combat vessels, including the super battleship *Yamato*. Postwar examination of Japanese records revealed that Japanese aircraft losses at Okinawa were far below often-repeated US estimates for the campaign. The number of conventional and kamikaze aircraft actually lost or expended by the 3rd, 5th, and 10th Air Fleets, combined with about 500 lost or expended by the Imperial Army at Okinawa, was roughly 1,430. The Allies destroyed 27 Japanese tanks and 743 artillery pieces (including mortars, anti-tank and anti-aircraft guns), some of them eliminated by the naval and air bombardments but most knocked out by American counter-battery fire.

**Figure 21:** *A group of Japanese prisoners taken on the island of Okuku in June 1945*

## Civilian losses, suicides, and atrocities

Some of the other islands that saw major battles in World War II, such as Iwo
Jima, were uninhabited or had been evacuated. Okinawa, by contrast, had
a large indigenous civilian population; US Army records from the planning
phase of the operation make the assumption that Okinawa was home to about
300,000 civilians. According to various estimates, between a tenth and a third
of them died during the battle, between 30,000 and 100,000. Okinawa Prefecture's estimate is over 100,000 losses, while the official US Army count for
the 82-day campaign is a total of 142,058 civilian casualties, including those
killed by artillery fire, air attacks, and those pressed into service by the Imperial
Japanese Army.

During the battle, American soldiers found it difficult to distinguish civilians
from soldiers. It became common for them to shoot at Okinawan houses, as
one infantryman wrote:

> *There was some return fire from a few of the houses, but the others were
> probably occupied by civilians – and we didn't care. It was a terrible thing
> not to distinguish between the enemy and women and children. Americans
> always had great compassion, especially for children. Now we fired in-
> discriminately.*[27]

**Figure 22:** *A US Marine Corps Stinson Sentinel observation plane flies over the razed Naha, capital of Okinawa, in May 1945.*

**Figure 23:** *Two US Marines share a foxhole with an Okinawan war orphan in April 1945.*

**Figure 24:** *Overcoming the civilian resistance on Okinawa was aided by US propaganda leaflets, one of which is being read by a prisoner awaiting transport.*

In its history of the war, the Okinawa Prefectural Peace Memorial Museum presents Okinawa as being caught between Japan and the United States. During the 1945 battle, the Imperial Japanese Army showed indifference to Okinawans' safety, and its soldiers even used civilians as human shields or just outright murdered them. The Japanese military confiscated food from the Okinawans and executed those who hid it, leading to mass starvation, and forced civilians out of their shelters. Japanese soldiers also killed about 1,000 people who spoke in the Okinawan language to suppress spying. The museum writes that "some were blown apart by [artillery] shells, some finding themselves in a hopeless situation were driven to suicide, some died of starvation, some succumbed to malaria, while others fell victim to the retreating Japanese troops."

With the impending Japanese defeat, civilians often committed mass suicide, urged on by the Japanese soldiers who told locals that victorious American soldiers would go on a rampage of killing and raping. *Ryūkyū Shimpō*, one of the two major Okinawan newspapers, wrote in 2007: "There are many Okinawans who have testified that the Japanese Army directed them to commit suicide. There are also people who have testified that they were handed grenades by Japanese soldiers" to blow themselves up. Thousands of civilians, having been induced by Japanese propaganda to believe that American soldiers were barbarians who committed horrible atrocities, killed their families and themselves to avoid capture. Some of them threw themselves and their family members from the southern cliffs where the Peace Museum now resides. Okinawans "were often surprised at the comparatively humane treatment they received from the American enemy". *Islands of Discontent: Okinawan Responses to Japanese and American Power* by Mark Selden notes that the Americans "did not pursue a policy of torture, rape, and murder of civilians as Japanese military officials had warned". American Military Intelligence Corps combat translators such as Teruto Tsubota managed to convince many civilians not to kill themselves.[28] Survivors of the mass suicides blamed also the indoctrination of their education system of the time, in which the Okinawans were taught to become "more Japanese than the Japanese", and were expected to prove it.

Witnesses and historians reported that soldiers, mainly Japanese troops, raped Okinawan women during the battle. Rape by Japanese troops "became common"Wikipedia:Attribution needed in June, after it became clear that the Imperial Japanese Army had been defeated. Marine Corps officials in Okinawa and Washington have said that they knew of no rapes by American personnel in Okinawa at the end of the war. There are, however, numerous credible testimony accounts which allege that a large number of rapes were committed by American forces during the battle. This includes claimed rape after trading sexual favors or even marrying Americans, such as the alleged incident in the village of Katsuyama, where civilians said they had formed a vigilante group to ambush and kill three black American soldiers whom they claimed would frequently rape the local girls there.

**MEXT controversy**

There is ongoing disagreement between Okinawa's local government and Japan's national government over the role of the Japanese military in civilian mass suicides during the battle. In March 2007, the national Ministry of Education, Culture, Sports, Science and Technology (MEXT) advised textbook publishers to reword descriptions that the embattled Imperial Japanese Army forced civilians to kill themselves in the war to avoid being taken prisoner. MEXT preferred descriptions that just say that civilians received hand grenades from the Japanese military. This move sparked widespread protests among Okinawans. In June 2007, the Okinawa Prefectural Assembly adopted a resolution stating, "We strongly call on the (national) government to retract the instruction and to immediately restore the description in the textbooks so the truth of the Battle of Okinawa will be handed down correctly and a tragic war will never happen again."[29]

On September 29, 2007, about 110,000 people held the biggest political rally in the history of Okinawa to demand that MEXT retract its order to textbook publishers regarding revising the account of the civilian suicides. The resolution stated, "It is an undeniable fact that the 'multiple suicides' would not

have occurred without the involvement of the Japanese military and any dele-
tion of or revision to (the descriptions) is a denial and distortion of the many
testimonies by those people who survived the incidents." In December 2007,
MEXT partially admitted the role of the Japanese military in civilian mass
suicides.[30] The ministry's Textbook Authorization Council allowed the publishers to reinstate the reference that civilians "were forced into mass suicides
by the Japanese military", on condition it is placed in sufficient context. The
council report stated, "It can be said that from the viewpoint of the Okinawa
residents, they were forced into the mass suicides."[31] That was not enough for
the survivors who said it is important for children today to know what really
happened.[32]

The Nobel Prize-winning author Kenzaburō Ōe wrote a booklet which states
that the mass suicide order was given by the military during the battle.[33] He
was sued by revisionists, including a wartime commander during the battle,
who disputed this and wanted to stop publication of the booklet. At a court
hearing, Ōe testified "Mass suicides were forced on Okinawa islanders under
Japan's hierarchical social structure that ran through the state of Japan, the
Japanese armed forces and local garrisons."[34] In March 2008, the Osaka Prefecture Court ruled in favor of Ōe, stating, "It can be said the military was
deeply involved in the mass suicides." The court recognized the military's involvement in the mass suicides and murder-suicides, citing the testimony about
the distribution of grenades for suicide by soldiers and the fact that mass suicides were not recorded on islands where the military was not stationed.[35]

In 2012, Korean-Japanese director Pak Su-nam announced her work on the
documentary *Nuchigafu* (Okinawan for "only if one is alive") collecting living
survivors' accounts to show "the truth of history to many people", alleging
that "there were two types of orders for 'honorable deaths'—one for residents
to kill each other and the other for the military to kill all residents".[36] In March
2013, Japanese textbook publisher Shimizu Shoin was permitted by MEXT to
publish the statements that "Orders from Japanese soldiers led to Okinawans
committing group suicide" and "The [Japanese] army caused many tragedies
in Okinawa, killing local civilians and forcing them to commit mass suicide."[37]

# Aftermath

Ninety percent of the buildings on the island were destroyed, along with count-
less historical documents, artifacts, and cultural treasures, and the tropical
landscape was turned into "a vast field of mud, lead, decay and maggots".[38]
The military value of Okinawa "exceeded all hope". Okinawa provided a fleet
anchorage, troop staging areas, and airfields in proximity to Japan. The US

**Figure 25:** *The Cornerstone of Peace Memorial with names of all military and civilians from all countries who died in the Battle of Okinawa*

**Figure 26:** *Marines celebrate Victory over Japan Day on Okinawa, August 1945*

cleared the surrounding waters of mines in Operation *Zebra*, occupied Okinawa, and set up the United States Civil Administration of the Ryukyu Islands, a form of military government, after the battle. In 2011, one official of the prefectural government told David Hearst of *The Guardian*:

> *You have the Battle of Britain, in which your airmen protected the British people. We had the Battle of Okinawa, in which the exact opposite happened. The Japanese army not only starved the Okinawans but used them as human shields. That dark history is still present today – and Japan and the US should study it before they decide what to do with next.*

## Effect on the wider war

Because the next major event following the Battle of Okinawa was "the total surrender of Japan," the "effect" of this battle is more difficult to consider. Due to the surrender, the next anticipated series of battles – an invasion of the Japanese homeland – never occurred. (Therefore, all military strategies on both sides which presupposed this apparently-inevitable next development were immediately rendered moot.)

Some military historians believe that the Okinawa campaign led directly to the atomic bombings of Hiroshima and Nagasaki, as a means of avoiding the planned ground invasion of the Japanese mainland. This view is explained by Victor Davis Hanson in his book *Ripples of Battle*:

> *... because the Japanese on Okinawa ... were so fierce in their defense (even when cut off, and without supplies), and because casualties were so appalling, many American strategists looked for an alternative means to subdue mainland Japan, other than a direct invasion. This means presented itself, with the advent of atomic bombs, which worked admirably in convincing the Japanese to sue for peace [unconditionally], without American casualties.*

Meanwhile, many parties continue to debate the broader question of "why Japan surrendered", attributing the surrender to a number of possible reasons including: the atomic bombings,[39] the Soviet invasion of Manchuria,[40,41] and Japan's depleted resources.Wikipedia:Citing sources[42]

## Memorial

In 1995, the Okinawa government erected a memorial monument named the Cornerstone of Peace in Mabuni, the site of the last fighting in southeastern Okinawa. The memorial lists all the known names of those who died in the battle, civilian and military, Japanese and foreign. As of June 2008, it contains 240,734 names.[43]

## Modern US base

Significant US forces remain garrisoned on Okinawa as the United States Forces Japan, which the Japanese government sees as an important guarantee of regional stability, and Kadena remains the largest US air base in Asia. Local residents have protested against the size and presence of the base.

# References

⊛ This article incorporates public domain material from websites or documents of the United States Army Center of Military History.

# Sources

### Secondary sources

<templatestyles src="Template:Refbegin/styles.css" />

- Appleman, Roy Edgar; Burns, James M.; Gugeler, Russel A.; Stevens, John (1948). *Okinawa: The Last Battle*[44]. Washington DC: United States Army Center of Military History. ISBN 1-4102-2206-3. full text online[45]
- Astor, Gerald (1996). *Operation Iceberg: The Invasion and Conquest of Okinawa in World War II*. Dell. ISBN 0-440-22178-1.
- Frank, Richard B. (1999). *Downfall: The End of the Imperial Japanese Empire*[46]. Random House. ISBN 978-0-679-41424-7.
- Feifer, George (2001). *The Battle of Okinawa: The Blood and the Bomb*. The Lyons Press. ISBN 1-58574-215-5.
- Fisch Jr., Arnold G. *Ryukyus*[47]. World War II Campaign Brochures. Washington D.C.: United States Army Center of Military History. ISBN 0-16-048032-9. CMH Pub 72-35.
- Gandt, Robert (2010). *The Twilight Warriors*. Broadway Books. ISBN 978-0-7679-3241-7.
- Hallas, James H. (2006). *Killing Ground on Okinawa: The Battle for Sugar Loaf Hill*. Potomac Books. ISBN 1-59797-063-8.
- Hastings, Max (2007). *Retribution – The Battle for Japan, 1944–45*. New York: Alfred A. Knopf. ISBN 978-0-307-26351-3.
- Hobbs, David (2012). *The British Pacific Fleet: The Royal Navy's Most Powerful Strike Force*. Seaforth Publishing. ISBN 9781783469222.
- Morison, Samuel Eliot (2002). *Victory in the Pacific, 1945,* vol. 14 of *History of United States Naval Operations in World War II*. Champaign, Illinois, USA: University of Illinois Press. ISBN 0-252-07065-8.
- Nichols, Charles Sidney; Henry I. Shaw Jr. (1989). *Okinawa: Victory in the Pacific*. Battery Press. ASIN B00071UAT8.

- Rottman, Gordon (2002). *Okinawa 1945: The last Battle*. Osprey Publishing. ISBN 1-84176-546-5.
- Sloan, Bill (2007). *The Ultimate Battle: Okinawa 1945—The Last Epic Struggle of World War II*. Simon & Schuster. ISBN 0-7432-9246-4.
- Zaloga, Steven J. *Japanese Tanks 1939–45*. Osprey, 2007. ISBN 978-1-84603-091-8.

## Primary sources

- Buckner, Simon Bolivar Jr. and Joseph Stilwell. *Seven Stars: The Okinawa Battle Diaries of Simon Bolivar Buckner, Jr. and Joseph Stilwell* ed. by Nicholas Evan Sarantakes (2004) excerpt and text search[48]
- Lacey, Laura Homan (2005). *Stay Off The Skyline: The Sixth Marine Division on Okinawa—An Oral History*. Potomac Books. ISBN 1-57488-952-4.
- Manchester, William (1980). *Goodbye, Darkness: A Memoir of the Pacific War*. Boston, Toronto: Little, Brown and Co. ISBN 0-316-54501-5.
- Sledge, E. B.; Fussell, Paul (1990). *With the Old Breed: At Peleliu and Okinawa*. Oxford University Press. ISBN 0-19-506714-2., famous Marine memoir
- Yahara, Hiromichi (2001). *The Battle for Okinawa*. John Wiley & Sons. ISBN 0-471-18080-7.-Firsthand account of the battle by a surviving Japanese officer.

# External links

> ⊙ Wikimedia Commons has media related to *Battle of Okinawa*.

- Dyer, George Carroll (1956). "The Amphibians Came to Conquer: The Story of Admiral Richmond Kelly Turner"[49]. United States Government Printing Office. Archived[50] from the original on May 21, 2011. Retrieved May 5, 2011.
- Huber, Thomas M. (May 1990). "Japan's Battle of Okinawa, April–June 1945"[51]. *Leavenworth Papers*. United States Army Command and General Staff College. Archived from the original[52] on December 16, 2006. Retrieved November 20, 2006.
- A film clip "footage from the National Archives.By Sgt. Rhodes"[53] is available at the Internet Archive
- A film clip "Landings On Okinawa, 1945/04/09 (1945)"[54] is available at the Internet Archive

- A film clip "Argentine Admitted To World Parley, 1945/05/03 (1945)"[55] is available at the Internet Archive
- A film clip "Final Days of Struggle in Okinawa, 1945/07/05 (1945)"[56] is available at the Internet Archive
- US military on the Battle of Okinawa[57]
- New Zealand account with reference to Operation *Iceberg*[58]
- Cornerstone of Peace[59]
- Okinawa Prefectural Peace Memorial Museum[60]
- The Peace Learning Archive in OKINAWA[61]
- A photographic record of aircraft carrier HMS *Indomitable*, 1944–45, including Operation Iceberg, the attack on the Sakashimas[62]
- WWII: Battle of Okinawa[63] – slideshow by *Life magazine*
- Operation Iceberg Operational Documents[64] Combined Arms Research Library, Fort Leavenworth, KS
- Oral history interview with Mike Busha, a member of the 6th Marine Division during the Battle of Okinawa[65] from the Veterans History Project at Central Connecticut State University
- Oral history interview with Albert D'Amico, a Navy Veteran who was aboard LST 278 during the landing at Okinawa[66] from the Veterans History Project at Central Connecticut State University
- *Booknotes* interview with Robert Leckie on *Okinawa: The Last Battle of World War II*, September 3, 1995.[67]

# Operation Ten-Go

## Operation Ten-Go

<table>
<tr><td colspan="2" align="center">**Operation Ten-Go**<br>天號作戰 or 天号作囗</td></tr>
<tr><td colspan="2" align="center">Part of the Battle of Okinawa, Pacific Theater, World War II</td></tr>
<tr><td colspan="2" align="center"><br><br>*Yamato* under attack. A large fire burns aft of her super-structure and she is low in the water from torpedo damage.</td></tr>
<tr><td align="right">**Date**</td><td>7 April 1945</td></tr>
<tr><td align="right">**Location**</td><td>Pacific Ocean, between Kyūshū, Japan, and Ryūkyū Islands</td></tr>
<tr><td align="right">**Result**</td><td>• American victory<br>• Destruction of the Japanese flagship.</td></tr>
<tr><td colspan="2" align="center">**Belligerents**</td></tr>
<tr><td>United States</td><td>● Empire of Japan</td></tr>
<tr><td colspan="2" align="center">**Commanders and leaders**</td></tr>
<tr><td>Marc Mitscher<br>Joseph J. Clark<br>Frederick C. Sherman</td><td>Seiichi Itō †<br>Keizō Komura<br>Kosaku Aruga †</td></tr>
<tr><td colspan="2" align="center">**Units involved**</td></tr>
<tr><td>U.S. 5th Fleet<br>• Task Force 58</td><td>Combined Fleet<br>• 2nd Fleet</td></tr>
<tr><td colspan="2" align="center">**Strength**</td></tr>
</table>

| 11 aircraft carriers<br>6 battleships<br>11 cruisers<br>30+ destroyers<br>386 carrier based aircraft | 1 battleship<br>1 light cruiser<br>8 destroyers<br>115 aircraft, mostly *kamikaze* |
|---|---|
| **Casualties and losses** | |
| Attack on *Yamato* task force: 12 aircrew dead<br>10 aircraft destroyed<br>In *kamikaze* attacks:<br>85 killed & missing<br>122 wounded<br>1 carrier moderately damaged<br>1 battleship moderately damaged<br>1 destroyer heavily damaged | Yamato task force: 3,700–4,250 dead[68]<br>1 battleship sunk<br>1 light cruiser sunk<br>4 destroyers sunk<br>1 destroyer heavily damaged<br>Kamikaze: 100 aircraft destroyed, 100+ dead |

**Operation Ten-Go** (天號作戰 (Kyūjitai) or 天号作□ (Shinjitai) *Ten-gō Sakusen*) was a Japanese naval operation plan in 1945, consisting of four likely scenarios. Its first scenario, **Operation Heaven One** (or **Ten-ichi-gō** 天一号 ) became the last major Japanese naval operation in the Pacific Theater of World War II. The resulting engagement is also known as the **Battle of the East China Sea**.

In April 1945, the Japanese battleship *Yamato* (the largest battleship in the world), along with nine other Japanese warships, embarked from Japan on a deliberate suicide attack upon Allied forces engaged in the Battle of Okinawa. The Japanese force was attacked, stopped, and almost destroyed by United States carrier-borne aircraft before reaching Okinawa. *Yamato* and five other Japanese warships were sunk.

The battle demonstrated U.S. air supremacy in the Pacific theater by this stage in the war and the vulnerability of surface ships without air cover to aerial attack. The battle also exhibited Japan's willingness to sacrifice entire ships, even the pride of its fleet, in desperate *kamikaze* attacks aimed at slowing the Allied advance on the Japanese home islands.

# Background

By early 1945, following the Solomon Islands campaign, the Battle of the Philippine Sea and the Battle of Leyte Gulf, the once-formidable Imperial Japanese Navy's Combined Fleet was reduced to just a handful of operational warships and a few remaining aircraft and aircrew. Most of the remaining Japanese warships in the Combined Fleet were stationed at ports in Japan, with most of the large ships at Kure, Hiroshima.[69]

As a final step before the planned invasion of the Japanese home islands, Allied forces invaded Okinawa on 1 April 1945. In March, in briefing Emperor Hirohito on Japan's response to the expected Okinawan invasion, Japanese military leaders explained that the Japanese Imperial Army was planning extensive air attacks, including the use of *kamikaze*. The emperor then reportedly asked, "But what about the Navy? What are they doing to assist in defending Okinawa? Have we no more ships?" Now feeling pressured by the emperor to also mount some kind of attack, Japan's Navy commanders conceived a *kamikaze*-type mission for their remaining operational large ships, which included the battleship *Yamato*.[70]

The resulting plan—drafted under the direction of the Commander-in-Chief of the Combined Fleet, Admiral Toyoda Soemu[71]—called for *Yamato* and her escorts to attack the U.S. fleet supporting the U.S. troops landing on the west of the island. *Yamato* and her escorts were to fight their way to Okinawa and then beach themselves between Higashi and Yomitan and fight as shore batteries until they were destroyed. Once the ships were destroyed, their surviving crewmembers were supposed to abandon ship and fight U.S. forces on land. Very little, if any, air cover could be provided for the ships, which would render them almost helpless to concentrated attacks from US carrier-based aircraft. In preparation for executing the plan, the assigned ships left Kure for Tokuyama, Yamaguchi, off Mitajiri, Japan, on 29 March.[72] However, despite obeying orders to prepare for the mission, Vice-Admiral Seiichi Itō—commander of the *Ten-Go* force—still refused to actually order his ships to carry it out, believing the plan to be futile and wasteful.[73]

Other commanders of the Imperial Japanese Navy also had very negative feelings about the operation, believing that it was a waste of human life and fuel. Captain Atsushi Ōi—who commanded escort fleets—was critical as fuel and resources were diverted from his operation. As he was told that the aim of this operation was "the tradition and the glory of Navy," he shouted:[74]

*This war is of our nation and why should the honor of our "surface fleet" be more respected? Who cares about their glory? Damn fools!*

*("Surface fleet" refers to capital ships, especially battleships that "should have won the war".)*

Vice Admiral Ryūnosuke Kusaka flew from Tokyo on 5 April to Tokuyama in a final attempt to convince the assembled commanders of the Combined Fleet—including Admiral Itō—to accept the plan. Upon first hearing of the proposed operation (it had been kept secret from most of them), the Combined Fleet commanders and captains unanimously joined Admiral Itō in rejecting it for the same reasons that he had expressed. Admiral Kusaka then explained that the Navy's attack would help divert U.S. aircraft away from the Army's planned kamikaze attacks on the U.S. fleet at Okinawa. He also explained that Japan's national leadership, including the emperor, were expecting the Navy to make their best effort to support the defense of Okinawa.

**Figure 27:** *Routes of the Japanese force (black line)*
*and U.S. carrier aircraft (red dash) to the battle area.*

Upon hearing this, the Combined Fleet commanders relented and accepted the proposed plan. The ships' crews were briefed on the nature of the mission and given the opportunity to stay behind if desired — none did. However, approximately 80 crew members who were new, sick, or infirm, were ordered off the ships, including sixty-seven naval cadets of Etajima Naval Academy Class No. 74 who had arrived on the battleship three days earlier.[75] The ships' crews now engaged in some last-minute intense drills to prepare for the mission, mostly practicing damage-control procedures.[76] At midnight, the ships were fueled. Reportedly, in secret defiance of orders to provide the ships with only just enough fuel to reach Okinawa, the Tokuyama personnel actually gave *Yamato* and the other ships almost all of the remaining fuel in the port, although this probably still was not enough to allow the force to return to Japan from Okinawa.[77] In a ceremonial farewell, officers and enlisted men drank sake together.

## Prelude

At 16:00 on 6 April, *Yamato*, with Admiral Itō on board, the light cruiser *Yahagi* and eight destroyers departed Tokuyama to begin the mission.[78] Two American submarines—*Threadfin* and *Hackleback*—sighted the Japanese force as it proceeded south through Bungo Suidō. Although they were unable to attack (due to the ships' speed), they did spend several hours shadowing the Japanese sortie and sending updates of its course to the U.S. fleet. The submarines' messages, which were reportedly sent uncoded, were also picked up by radio operators on the Japanese ships.[79]

At dawn on 7 April, the Japanese force passed the Ōsumi Peninsula into the open ocean heading south from Kyūshū toward Okinawa. They shifted into a defensive formation, with *Yahagi* leading *Yamato* and the eight destroyers deployed in a ring around the two larger ships, with each ship 1,500 m (1,600 yd) from each other and proceeding at 20 kn (23 mph; 37 km/h).[80] One of the Japanese destroyers—*Asashimo*—developed engine trouble and turned back. U.S. reconnaissance aircraft began to shadow the main force of ships. At 10:00, the Japanese force turned west to make it look like they were withdrawing, but at 11:30, after being detected by two American PBM Mariner flying boats, the *Yamato* fired a salvo with her 460 mm (18.1 in) bow guns using special "beehive shells" (三式焼霰□, *san-shiki shōsan dan*) but could not prevent the two planes from shadowing the Japanese force, they turned back towards Okinawa.

Upon receiving contact reports early on 7 April, U.S. 5th Fleet commander Admiral Raymond Spruance ordered Task Force 54, which consisted mostly of modernized Standard-type battleships under the command of Admiral Morton Deyo (which were engaged in shore bombardment), to intercept and destroy the Japanese sortie. Deyo moved to execute his orders, but Vice Admiral Marc A. Mitscher, who commanded Task Force 58 (TF 58), preempted Spruance and Deyo by launching a massive air strike from his carriers, without informing Spruance until after the launches were completed.[81] As a senior naval aviation officer, "Mitscher had spent a career fighting the battleship admirals who had steered the navy's thinking for most of the current century. One of those was his immediate superior, Raymond Spruance. Mitscher felt a stirring of battleship versus aircraft carrier rivalry. Though the carriers had mostly fought the great battles of the Pacific, whether air power alone could prevail over a surface force had not been proven beyond all doubt. Here was an opportunity to end the debate forever".

Around 10:00 on 7 April, Task Groups 58.1 and 58.3 (TG 58.1 and 58.3) began launching almost 400 aircraft in several waves from eight carriers (TG 58.1: *Hornet, Bennington, Belleau Wood, San Jacinto*; TG 58.3 *Essex, Bunker Hill, Hancock* and *Bataan*) that were located just east of Okinawa. The aircraft consisted of F6F Hellcat and F4U Corsair fighters, SB2C Helldiver dive bombers, and TBF Avenger torpedo bombers. After being informed of Mitscher's launches, Spruance agreed that the airstrikes could go ahead as planned. As a contingency, Spruance ordered Admiral Deyo to assemble a force of six battleships (*Massachusetts, Indiana, New Jersey, South Dakota,*

**Figure 28:** *U.S. aircraft, such as this Curtiss SB2C-3 Helldiver, begin their attacks on Yamato (center left). A Japanese destroyer is in the center right of the picture.*[84]

*Wisconsin*, and *Missouri*), together with seven cruisers (including the large cruisers *Alaska* and *Guam*) and 21 destroyers, and to prepare for a surface engagement with *Yamato* should the airstrikes prove unsuccessful.[82,83]

# Battle

Around 12:00, the first American aircraft arrived over *Yamato*; these were F6F Hellcat and F4U Corsair fighters, which were under orders to deal with any Japanese aircraft that might appear to defend the ships below. None did.[85]

Since it soon became obvious that the Japanese force had no air cover, the U.S. aircraft were able to set up for their attacks without fear of opposition from Japanese aircraft. U.S. bomber and torpedo aircraft arriving over the *Yamato* group—after their two-hour flight from Okinawa—were thus able to circle the Japanese ship formation just out of anti-aircraft range in order to methodically set up their attacks on the warships below. The first wave of U.S. carrier planes were spotted by a Japanese lookout on the bridge at 12:32. Two minutes later, Yamato opened fire with her 460 mm main batteries. The Japanese ships stopped zigzagging and increased speed to 24 kn (28 mph; 44 km/h), beginning evasive maneuvers, and opened fire with their anti-aircraft guns. *Yamato* carried almost 150 anti-aircraft guns, including her massive 460 mm guns.[86]

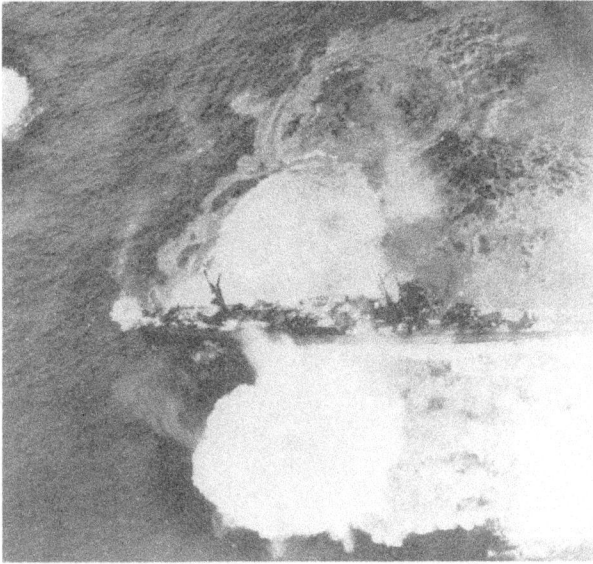

**Figure 29:** *The light cruiser Yahagi under intense bomb and torpedo attack.*[88]

The American F6F Hellcat fighters "were supposed to go first, strafing, rock-eting, dropping light ordnance, distracting the enemy gunners while the SB2C Helldivers plunged almost straight down with their heavy bombs". This was because the TBM Avenger torpedo bombers "needed all the distraction and diversion they could get when they made their dangerous low altitude runs straight at the enemy ships". The Avengers mainly attacked from the port side so that if the torpedoes hit that side, it would increase the likelihood of the target ship capsizing.[87]

At 12:46, a torpedo hit *Yahagi* directly in her engine room, killing the entire engineering room crew and bringing her to a complete stop. *Yahagi* was hit by at least six more torpedoes and 12 bombs by succeeding waves of air attacks. The Japanese destroyer *Isokaze* attempted to come to *Yahagi*'s aid but was attacked and heavily damaged, and sank sometime later. *Yahagi* capsized and sank at 14:05.[89]

During the first attack wave, despite evasive maneuvers that caused most of the bombs and torpedoes aimed at her to miss, *Yamato* was hit by two armor-piercing bombs and one torpedo.[90] Her speed was not affected, but one of the bombs started a fire aft of the superstructure that was not extinguished. Also, during the first attack wave, Japanese destroyers *Hamakaze* and *Suzutsuki* were heavily damaged and taken out of the battle. *Hamakaze* sank later.

**Figure 30:** *Yamato listing to port and on fire*

Between 13:20 and 14:15, the second and third waves of U.S. aircraft attacked, concentrating on *Yamato*. During this time, *Yamato* was hit by at least eight torpedoes and up to 15 bombs. The bombs did extensive damage to the topside of the ship, including knocking out power to the gun directors and forcing the anti-aircraft guns to be individually and manually aimed and fired, greatly reducing their effectiveness.[91] The torpedo hits—almost all on the port side—caused *Yamato* to list enough that capsizing was now an imminent danger.[92] The water damage-control station had been destroyed by a bomb hit making it impossible to counter-flood the specially designed spaces within the ship's hull to counteract hull damage. At 13:33, in a desperate attempt to keep the ship from capsizing, *Yamato*'s damage control team counter-flooded both starboard engine and boiler rooms. This mitigated the danger but also drowned the several hundred crewmen manning those stations, who were given no notice that their compartments were about to fill with water.[93,94] The loss of the starboard engines—plus the weight of the water—caused *Yamato* to slow to about 10 kn (12 mph; 19 km/h).[95] At that same moment, the Americans launched another 110 aircraft from Task Group 58. Twenty Avengers made a new torpedo run from 60 degrees to port. Yamato started a sharp turn to port but three torpedoes ripped into her port side amidships, jamming her auxiliary rudder in position hard port.[96]

**Figure 31:** *The only known photo of the Yamato explod-ing. The ship capsized after numerous bomb and torpedo hits.*

With *Yamato* proceeding more slowly and therefore easier to target, U.S. tor-pedo aircraft concentrated on hitting her rudder and stern with torpedoes in order to affect her steering ability, which they succeeded in doing.[97] At 14:02, after being informed that the ship could no longer steer and was unavoidably sinking, Admiral Itō ordered the mission canceled, the crew to abandon ship, and for the remaining ships to begin rescuing survivors. *Yamato* communi-cated this message to the other surviving ships by signal flag because her radios had been destroyed.[98]

At 14:05, *Yamato* was stopped dead in the water and began to capsize. Admiral Itō and Captain Aruga refused to abandon her with the rest of the survivors. At 14:20, *Yamato* capsized completely and began to sink ( 30°22′N 128°04′E[99]). At 14:23, she suddenly blew up with an explosion so large that it was reportedly heard and seen 200 km (110 nmi; 120 mi) away in Kagoshima and sent up a mushroom-shaped cloud almost 20,000 ft (6,100 m) into the air.[100] Japanese survivor Yoshida Mitsuru said that her large explosion downed several U.S. planes observing her end. The explosion is believed to have occurred when the fires ignited by bomb hits reached the main magazines.[101]

Attempting to make it back to port, Japanese destroyer *Asashimo* was bombed and sunk with all hands by U.S. aircraft. The Japanese destroyer *Kasumi* was

**Figure 32:** *Yamato moments after exploding.*

also crippled by U.S. carrier aircraft attack during the battle and had to be scuttled by other, relatively undamaged Japanese destroyers. *Suzutsuki*—despite her bow being blown off—was able to make it to Sasebo, Japan, by steaming in reverse the entire way.

The remaining three less-damaged Japanese destroyers (*Fuyutsuki*, *Yukikaze*, and *Hatsushimo*) were able to rescue 280 survivors from *Yamato* (sources differ on the size of *Yamato*'s crew, giving it as between 2,750 and 3,300 men), plus 555 survivors from *Yahagi* (out of a crew of 1,000) and just over 800 survivors from *Isokaze*, *Hamakaze*, and *Kasumi*. Between 3,700 and 4,250 Japanese naval personnel perished in the battle.[102] The ships took the survivors to Sasebo.[103]

A total of 10 U.S. aircraft were shot down by anti-aircraft fire from the Japanese ships; some of the aircrews were rescued by seaplane or submarine. In total, the U.S. lost 12 men. Some of the Japanese survivors reported that U.S. fighter aircraft machine-gunned Japanese survivors floating in the water.[104,105] Japanese survivors also reported that U.S. aircraft temporarily halted their attacks on the Japanese destroyers during the time that the destroyers were busy picking up survivors from the water.[106]

## Aerial kamikaze attacks

During the battle, the Japanese Army conducted an air attack on the U.S. naval fleet at Okinawa as promised, but they failed to sink any ships. Around 115 aircraft—many of them *kamikaze*—attacked the U.S. ships throughout the day of 7 April. *Kamikaze* aircraft hit the aircraft carrier *Hancock*, battleship *Maryland*, and destroyer *Bennett*, causing moderate damage to *Hancock* and *Maryland* and heavy damage to *Bennett*. About 100 of the Japanese aircraft were lost in the attack.[107]

# Aftermath

*Ten-Go* was the last major Japanese naval operation of the war, and the remaining Japanese warships had little involvement in combat operations for the rest of the conflict. *Suzutsuki* was never repaired. *Fuyuzuki* was repaired but hit a U.S. air-dropped mine at Moji, Japan, on 20 August 1945, and was not subsequently repaired. *Yukikaze* survived the war almost undamaged. *Hatsushimo* hit a U.S. air-dropped mine on 30 July 1945, near Maizuru, Japan, and was the 129th, and last, Japanese destroyer sunk in the war.[108]

*Maryland* was kept out of the war following the *kamikaze* attacks.

Okinawa was declared secure by Allied forces on 21 June 1945,[109] after an intense and costly battle. Japan surrendered in August 1945, after being bombed twice with atomic weapons. The apparent willingness of Japan to sacrifice so many of its people using suicidal tactics such as Operation *Ten-Go* and in the Battle of Okinawa reportedly was a factor in the American decision to employ atomic weapons against Japan.[110]

The story of Operation *Ten-Go* is revered to some degree in modern Japan as evidenced by appearances of the story in popular Japanese culture which usually portray the event as a brave, selfless, but futile, symbolic effort by the participating Japanese sailors to defend their homeland. One of the reasons the event may have such significance in Japanese culture is that the word *Yamato* was often used as a poetic name for Japan. Thus, the end of battleship *Yamato* could serve as a metaphor for the end of the Japanese empire.[111,112]

# References

<templatestyles src="Template:Refbegin/styles.css" />

* Feifer, George (2001). "Operation Heaven Number One". *The Battle of Okinawa: The Blood and the Bomb*. The Lyons Press. ISBN 1-58574-215-5.

- Garzke, William H.; Dulin, Robert O. (1985). *Battleships: Axis and Neutral Battleships in World War II*. Annapolis, Maryland: Naval Institute Press. ISBN 0-87021-101-3. OCLC 12613723[113].
- Hara, Tameichi (1961). "The Last Sortie". *Japanese Destroyer Captain*. New York & Toronto: Ballantine Books. ISBN 0-345-27894-1. A first-hand account of the battle by the captain of the Japanese cruiser *Yahagi*.
- Jentschura, Hansgeorg; Jung, Dieter; Mickel, Peter (1977). *Warships of the Imperial Japanese Navy, 1869-1945*. Annapolis, Maryland: United States Naval Institute. ISBN 0-87021-893-X.
- Ōi, Atsushi (1992). *Kaijo Goeisen*. Asahi Sonorama. ISBN 4-05-901040-5.
- Skulski, Janusz (1989). *The Battleship Yamato*. Annapolis, Maryland: Naval Institute Press. ISBN 0-87021-019-X.
- Spurr, Russell (1995). *A Glorious Way to Die: The Kamikaze Mission of the Battleship Yamato, April 1945*. Newmarket Press. ISBN 1-55704-248-9.
- Yoshida, Mitsuru; Minear, Richard H. (1999). *Requiem for Battleship Yamato*. Annapolis, Maryland: Naval Institute Press. ISBN 1-55750-544-6. A first-hand account of the battle by *Yamato*'s only surviving bridge officer.

# External links

> Wikimedia Commons has media related to *Operation Ten-Go*.

- "navweaps.com: Order of Battle"[114].
- "CombinedFleet.com: Chronological history of Yamato and actions during Ten-Go"[115].
- "NOVA documentary: Sinking the Supership"[116]. The official site of the NOVA documentary with additional information on the subject.

<indicator name="featured-star"> ⭐ </indicator>

# Appendix

## References

[1] //tools.wmflabs.org/geohack/geohack.php?pagename=Battle_of_Okinawa&params=26.5_N_ 128_E_type:isle_region:JP-46_source:dewiki

[2] Bill Sloan: The Ultimate Battle pg. 18

[3] Keegan: The Second World War pg. 567

[4] Hastings: Retribution pg. 370

[5] http://www.pref.okinawa.jp/site/kodomo/heiwadanjo/heiwa/7812.html

[6] Keegan: *The Times Atlas of the Second World War* pg. 169

[7] The National Archives: Heroes and Villains https://www.nationalarchives.gov.uk/education/ heroesvillains/background/g5_background.htm. Retrieved July 22, 2015.

[8] William T. Garner: *Unwavering Valor* ch. 12.

[9] Frank 1999, p. 71.

[10] "The Second World Wars: How the First Global Conflict Was Fought and Won" p. 302

[11] Garner: *Unwavering Valor* ch. 12.

[12] Keegan: The Second World War pg. 573

[13] "The Battle of Okinawa" http://www.history.com/topics/world-war-ii/battle-of-okinawa, Retrieved December 28, 2015.

[14] "The Cornerstone of Peace." Kyushu-Okinawa Summit 2000: Okinawa G8 Summit Host Preparation Council, 2000. Retrieved December 9, 2012.

[15] Giangreco *Hell to Pay* (2009) pg. 91

[16] The Last Battle pp. 91-92 https://history.army.mil/books/wwii/okinawa/chapter4.htm Retrieved 11/20/2017

[17] Feifer 2001 pages 99-106

[18] At 60th anniversary, Battle of Okinawa survivors recall 'Typhoon of Steel' - News - Stripes http://www.stripes.com/news/at-60th-anniversary-battle-of-okinawa-survivors-recall-typhoon-of-steel-1.31175, Allen, David; Stars and Stripes; April 1, 2005.

[19] Huber, Thomas M., Command and General Staff College

[20] John Toland, *The Rising Sun: The Decline and Fall of the Japanese Empire 1936–1945*, Random House, 1970, p. 711.

[21] Baldwin, Hanson W. *Sea Fights and Shipwrecks* Hanover House 1956 page 309

[22] Christopher Chant, "The Encyclopedia of Codenames of World War II (Routledge Revivals)", p. 87

[23] West Point Atlas of American Wars

[24] Battle of Okinawa http://www.globalsecurity.org/military/facility/okinawa-battle.htm, GlobalSecurity.org.

[25] John Toland, *The Rising Sun: The Decline and Fall of the Japanese Empire 1936–1945*, p. 723.

[26] Reid, Chip. "Ernie Pyle, trail-blazing war correspondent—Brought home the tragedy of D-Day and the rest of WWII" http://www.msnbc.msn.com/id/5130777/, *NBC News*, June 7, 2004. Retrieved April 26, 2006.

[27] Feifer, George, *The Battle of Okinawa*, The Lyons Press (2001), p. 374.

[28] Defiant soldier saved lives of hundreds of civilians during Okinawa battle http://www.stripes.com/news/defiant-soldier-saved-lives-of-hundreds-of-civilians-during-okinawa-battle-1.31173, *Stars and Stripes*, April 1, 2005.

[29] Okinawa slams history text rewrite http://search.japantimes.co.jp/cgi-bin/nn20070623a1.html, *Japan Times*, June 23, 2007.

[30] Japan to amend textbook accounts of Okinawa suicides http://www.iht.com/articles/2007/12/ 26/asia/japan.php *Herald Tribune*, December 26, 2007.

[31] Texts reinstate army's role in mass suicides: Okinawa prevails in history row http://search.japantimes.co.jp/cgi-bin/nn20071227a1.html *Japan Times*, December 27, 2007.

[32] Okinawa's war time wounds reopened http://news.bbc.co.uk/2/hi/asia-pacific/7098876.stm BBC News, November 17, 2007.

[33] Witness: Military ordered mass suicides http://search.japantimes.co.jp/cgi-bin/nn20070912a3.html, *Japan Times*, September 12, 2007.

[34] Oe testifies military behind Okinawa mass suicides http://search.japantimes.co.jp/cgi-bin/nn20071110a3.html , *Japan Times*, November 10, 2007.

[35] Court sides with Oe over mass suicides http://search.japantimes.co.jp/cgi-bin/nn20080329a1.html, *Japan Times*, March 29, 2008.

[36] Nayoki Himeno, Director humanizes tragedy of Okinawan mass suicides http://ajw.asahi.com/article/behind_news/social_affairs/AJ201205240011 , *The Asashi Shimbun*, May 24, 2012.

[37] New high school texts say Japanese Imperial Army ordered WWII Okinawa suicides https://archive.is/20130413130816/http://mainichi.jp/english/english/newsselect/news/20130327p2a00m0na014000c.html, *The Mainichi*, March 29, 2013.

[38] Okinawan History and Karate-do http://www.nyc-shorinryu.com/okinawa.html

[39] Frank 1999, p. 331.

[40] "Soviets declare war on Japan; invade Manchuria". http://www.history.com/this-day-in-history/soviets-declare-war-on-japan-invade-manchuria History.com. A&E Television Networks, n.d. Web. July 6, 2014.

[41] "Did Nuclear Weapons Cause Japan to Surrender?". https://m.youtube.com/watch?v=CSSexxwDzgs Wilson, Ward. YouTube. Carnegie Council for Ethics in International Affairs, January 16, 2013. Web. July 6, 2014.

[42] "Why did Japan surrender?" http://archive.boston.com/bostonglobe/ideas/articles/2011/08/07/why_did_japan_surrender/. Boston.com. August 7, 2011.

[43] Okinawa is promised reduced base burden http://search.japantimes.co.jp/cgi-bin/nn20080624a6.html, *The Japan Times*, June 24, 2008

[44] http://www.history.army.mil/books/wwii/okinawa/index.htm

[45] http://www.ibiblio.org/hyperwar/USA/USA-P-Okinawa/index.html

[46] https://books.google.com/books?id=cJXtAAAAMAAJ

[47] http://www.history.army.mil/brochures/ryukyus/ryukyus.htm

[48] https://www.amazon.com/dp/1585442941

[49] http://www.ibiblio.org/hyperwar/USN/ACTC/index.html

[50] https://web.archive.org/web/20110521010748/http://ibiblio.org/hyperwar/USN/ACTC/index.html

[51] https://web.archive.org/web/20061216035903/http://www-cgsc.army.mil/carl/resources/csi/Huber/Huber.asp

[52] http://www-cgsc.army.mil/carl/resources/csi/Huber/Huber.asp

[53] https://archive.org/details/gov.archives.li.127-g-1930

[54] https://archive.org/details/1945-04-09_Landings_On_Okinawa

[55] https://archive.org/details/1945-05-03_Argentine_Admitted_To_World_Parley

[56] https://archive.org/details/1945-07-05_Final_Days_of_Struggle_in_Okinawa

[57] http://www.history.army.mil/books/wwii/okinawa/

[58] http://www.nzetc.org/tm/scholarly/tei-WH2Navy-c24.html

[59] https://web.archive.org/web/20120606184144/http://www.pref.okinawa.jp/summit/a_la/peace/ishiji/index2.htm

[60] http://www.peace-museum.pref.okinawa.jp/english/index.html

[61] http://peacelearning.jp/

[62] http://www.naval-history.net/WW2Memoir-Indomitable-Whiteing4.htm

[63] http://www.life.com/image/first/in-gallery/41302/wwii-battle-of-okinawa

[64] http://cgsc.cdmhost.com/cdm4/results.php?CISOOP4=all&CISOFIELD4=CISOSEARCHALL&CISOBOX4=iceberg&c=all&CISOROOT=%2Fp4013coll8

[65] http://content.library.ccsu.edu/u?/VHP,5460

[66] http://content.library.ccsu.edu/u?/VHP,5592

[67] http://www.c-span.org/video/?66766-1/book-discussion-okinawa-last-battle-world-war-ii

[68] Jentshura and CombinedFleet.com. Abe, Saburo, *Tokko Yamato Kantai* (*The Special Attack Fleet Yamato*)", Kasumi Syuppan Co. 1995, a Japanese book which has apparently not been translated into English, gives the following breakdown in deaths for the Japanese in the operation: *Yamato*

– 3056 killed, 276 survivors; *Yahagi* – 446 killed; *Isokaze* – 20 killed; *Hamakaze* – 100 killed; *Yukikaze* – 3 killed; *Kasumi* – 17 killed; *Asashimo* – 326 killed (all hands); *Fuyuzuki* – 12 killed; *Suzutsuki* – 57 killed.

[69] Hara, *Japanese Destroyer Captain*, 274.

[70] Feifer, *The Battle of Okinawa*, 7.

[71] Minear, *Requiem*, xiii.

[72] Yoshida, *Requiem*, 6–7.

[73] Yoshida, *Requiem*, 62.

[74] Atsushi Ōi, *Kaijō Goeisen.*

[75] Hara, *Japanese Destroyer Captain*, 277.

[76] Yoshida, *Requiem*, 15.

[77] Spurr, *A Glorious Way to Die*, 162–165.

[78] Yoshida, *Requiem*, 30.

[79] Skulski, *The Battleship Yamato*, 12. The eight Japanese destroyers involved in the operation were: , , , , , and .

[80] Yoshida, *Requiem*, 47–49.

[81] *Triumph in the Pacific* by E.B. Potter, also *History of United States Naval Operations in World War II* by Samuel Eliot Morison.

[82] Order of Battle - Final Sortie of the Imperial Japanese Navy - 7 April 1945 http://navweaps. com/index_oob/OOB_WWII_Pacific/OOB_WWII_Final_Sortie.htm

[83] Authors Garzke and Dulin speculate that the likely outcome of a battle between these two surface forces would have been a victory for the Allies, but at a serious cost due to the large margin of superiority *Yamato* held over the American battleships in firepower (460 mm vs. 356 mm), armour and speed ( vs. (Garzke and Dulin (1985)), p. 60.

[84] Nova: *Sinking the Supership.*

[85] Garzke and Dulin (1985), pp. 60–61.

[86] Yoshida, *Requiem*, 62–64.

[87] Yoshida, *Requiem*, 74.

[88] CombinedFleet.com

[89] Hara, *Japanese Destroyer Captain*, 298.

[90] Yoshida, *Requiem*, 66.

[91] Yoshida, *Requiem*, 78.

[92] Yoshida, *Requiem*, 80.

[93] Yoshida, *Requiem*, 82.

[94] Feifer, *The Battle of Okinawa*, 17–25.

[95] Yoshida, *Requiem*, 83.

[96] http://www.combinedfleet.com/yamato.htm

[97] Yoshida, *Requiem*, 95–96.

[98] Yoshida, *Requiem*, 108.

[99] //tools.wmflabs.org/geohack/geohack.php?pagename=Operation_Ten-Go&params=30_22_N_128_04_E_type:event

[100] Yoshida, *Requiem*, 118.

[101] Skulski, *The Battleship Yamato*, 13.

[102] Jentshura, p. 39 says that 2,498 *Yamato* crewmen died. CombinedFleet.com says 3,063 on *Yamato* died. One possible reason for part of the discrepancy in the numbers is that Admiral Itō's staff may not have been included in the total ship's complement. Abe, Saburo, *Tokko Yamato Kantai (The Special Attack Fleet Yamato)*", Kasumi Syuppan Co. 1995, gives the following breakdown in deaths for the Japanese in the operation: *Yamato*- 3056 killed, 276 survivors; *Yahagi*- 446 killed; *Isokaze*- 20 killed; *Hamakaze*- 100 killed; *Yukikaze*- 3 killed; *Kasumi*- 17 killed; *Asashimo*- 326 killed (all hands); *Fuyuzuki*- 12 killed; *Suzutsuki*- 57 killed.

[103] Yoshida, *Requiem*, 140.

[104] "Then the Americans started to shoot with machine guns at the people who were floating, so we all had to dive under."

[105] Hara, *Japanese Destroyer Captain*, 301.

[106] Yoshida, *Requiem*, 144.

[107] Hara, *Japanese Destroyer Captain*, 304.

[108] Hara, *Japanese Destroyer Captain*, 281.

[109] Minear, *Requiem*, xiv.

[110] Feifer, *The Battle of Okinawa*, 410–430.

[111] Minear, *Requiem*, xvii.

[112] Jiji Press, " Yamato survivor, 87, recalls doomed mission http://www.japantimes.co.jp/news/ 2015/08/20/national/history/yamato-survivor-87-recalls-doomed-mission/", *Japan Times*, 20 August 2015

[113] //www.worldcat.org/oclc/12613723

[114] http://www.navweaps.com/index_oob/OOB_WWII_Pacific/OOB_WWII_Final_Sortie.htm

[115] http://www.combinedfleet.com/yamato.htm

[116] https://www.pbs.org/wgbh/nova/supership/

# Article Sources and Contributors

The sources listed for each article provide more detailed licensing information including the copyright status, the copyright owner, and the license conditions.

# Image Sources, Licenses and Contributors

The sources listed for each image provide more detailed licensing information including the copyright status, the copyright owner, and the license conditions.

**Image** *Source:* https://en.wikipedia.org/w/index.php?title=File:Ww2_158.jpg *License:* Public Domain *Contributors:* Staff Sergent Walter F. Kleine 1

**Image** *Source:* https://en.wikipedia.org/w/index.php?title=File:Flag_of_the_United_States_(1912-1959).svg *License:* Public Domain *Contributors:* Created by jacobolus using Adobe Illustrator. .................................................................................1

**Image** *Source:* https://en.wikipedia.org/w/index.php?title=File:Flag_of_the_United_Kingdom.svg *License:* Public Domain *Contributors:* Anomie, Good Olfactory, Jo-Jo Eumerus, MSGJ, Mifter ........................................................................1

**Image** *Source:* https://en.wikipedia.org/w/index.php?title=File:Canadian_Red_Ensign_(1921-1957).svg *License:* Public Domain *Contributors:* User:Denelson83 ..............................................................................1

**Image** *Source:* https://en.wikipedia.org/w/index.php?title=File:Flag_of_New_Zealand.svg *License:* Public Domain *Contributors:* Achim1999, Adabow, Adambro, Arria Belli, Avenue, Bawolff, Bjankuloski06en, ButterStick, Cycn, Denelson83, Denniss, Donk~commonswiki, Duduziq, EugeneZelenko, Fred J, FreshCorp619, Fry1989, George Ho, GoldenRainbow, Hugh Jass, Ibagli, Jusjih, Klemen Kocjancic, MAXXX-309, Mamndassan, Mattes, Mindmatrix, Nightstallion, O, Ozgurnarin, Peeperman, Pembe karadeniz, Poco a poco, Poromiami, Reisio, Rfc1394, Salvabl, Salvaeditor, Sarang, Shizhao, SiBr4, Steinsplitter, Tabasco~commonswiki, TintoMeches, Transparent Blue, Voyager, Väsk, Xufanc, Yann, Zscout370, 43 anonymous edits ........ 1

**Image** *Source:* https://en.wikipedia.org/w/index.php?title=File:Flag_of_Australia.svg *License:* Public Domain *Contributors:* Anomie, Jo-Jo Eumerus, Mifter ..........................................................................1

**Image** *Source:* https://en.wikipedia.org/w/index.php?title=File:Merchant_flag_of_Japan_(1870).svg *Contributors:* - ..................................1

**Image** *Source:* https://en.wikipedia.org/w/index.php?title=File:War_flag_of_the_Imperial_Japanese_Army.svg *License:* Public Domain *Contributors:* Thommy .................................................................................2

**Image** *Source:* https://en.wikipedia.org/w/index.php?title=File:Naval_ensign_of_the_Empire_of_Japan.svg *License:* Creative Commons Attribution-Sharealike 3.0 *Contributors:* Alkari, FDRMRZUSA, Fry1989, Illegitimate Barrister, Morio, NuclearElevator, 2 anonymous edits ....................2

**Image** *Source:* https://en.wikipedia.org/w/index.php?title=File:US_Tenth_Army_SSI.svg *License:* Creative Commons Attribution-Sharealike 3.0 *Contributors:* User:Fred the Oyster ............................................................................2

**Image** *Source:* https://en.wikipedia.org/w/index.php?title=File:XXIV_Corps_SSI.gif *License:* Public Domain *Contributors:* File Upload Bot (Magnus Manske), Illegitimate Barrister, Nobunaga24, OgreBot 2 .................................................2

**Image** *Source:* https://en.wikipedia.org/w/index.php?title=File:IIIMEFLogo.jpg *License:* Public Domain *Contributors:* FieldMarine, GrummelJS, Joey-das-WBF, KTo288, Los688, Sanandros, Tokorokoko ...................................................2

**Image** *Source:* https://en.wikipedia.org/w/index.php?title=File:United_States_Fifth_Fleet_insignia_2006.png *License:* Public Domain *Contributors:* Cobatfor, OgreBot 2, Stewi101015 .......................................................2

**Figure 1** *Source:* https://en.wikipedia.org/w/index.php?title=File:Battle_of_Okinawa.svg *License:* GNU Free Documentation License *Contributors:* BrokenSphere, MGA73bot2, Raul654, 1 anonymous edits ..................................................4

**Figure 2** *Source:* https://en.wikipedia.org/w/index.php?title=File:Japanese_Commanders_on_Okinawa.jpg *License:* Public Domain *Contributors:* User:W.wolny .................................................................................6

**Figure 3** *Source:* https://en.wikipedia.org/w/index.php?title=File:Childsoldier_In_Okinawa.jpg *License:* Public Domain *Contributors:* GENTOS, Hilohello, Kugel~commonswiki, Yaniv 01 ...........................................................8

**Figure 4** *Source:* https://en.wikipedia.org/w/index.php?title=File:Ie_defence_positions.png *License:* Public Domain *Contributors:* United States Army (Post-Work: User:W.wolny) ......................................................8

**Figure 5** *Source:* https://en.wikipedia.org/w/index.php?title=File:150-mm-japanese-gun-okinawa.jpg *License:* Public Domain *Contributors:* USMC .................................................................................8

**Figure 6** *Source:* https://en.wikipedia.org/w/index.php?title=File:Okinawa_airfields_1945.png *License:* Public Domain *Contributors:* USAAF .9

**Figure 7** *Source:* https://en.wikipedia.org/w/index.php?title=File:USS_Bunker_Hill_hit_by_two_Kamikazes.jpg *License:* Public Domain *Contributors:* U.S. Navy; .................................................................................10

**Figure 8** *Source:* https://en.wikipedia.org/w/index.php?title=File:HMS_Implacable_AWM_019037.jpg *License:* Public Domain *Contributors:* James Fitzpatrick ............................................................................11

**Figure 9** *Source:* https://en.wikipedia.org/w/index.php?title=File:Yamato_battleship_explosion.jpg *License:* Public Domain *Contributors:* Unknown US Navy personnel ......................................................12

**Figure 10** *Source:* https://en.wikipedia.org/w/index.php?title=File:HMS_Formidable_(67)_on_fire_1945.jpg *License:* Public Domain *Contributors:* Royal Navy official photographer aboard HMS Victorious (R38) .....................................13

**Figure 11** *Source:* https://en.wikipedia.org/w/index.php?title=File:New_Mexico_class_battleship_bombarding_Okinawa.jpg *License:* Public Domain *Contributors:* United States Navy photograph, photographed from USS West Virginia (BB-48). ..............................14

**Figure 12** *Source:* https://en.wikipedia.org/w/index.php?title=File:Marines_land_on_Okinawa_shores.jpg *License:* Public Domain *Contributors:* User:W.wolny .................................................................................15

**Figure 13** *Source:* https://en.wikipedia.org/w/index.php?title=File:OkinawaMarinesDeadJapanese.jpg *License:* Public Domain *Contributors:* ArjanH, Cla68, High Contrast, Movieevery, 1 anonymous edits ............................................16

**Figure 14** *Source:* https://en.wikipedia.org/w/index.php?title=File:OkinawaMarineCaveDemolition.jpg *License:* Public Domain *Contributors:* BotMultichill, BotMultichillT, Cla68, Movieevery, 1 anonymous edits .....................................17

**Figure 15** *Source:* https://en.wikipedia.org/w/index.php?title=File:Americans_on_Okinawa_hear_of_victory_in_Europe.jpg *License:* Public Domain *Contributors:* User:W.wolny .................................................................................17

**Figure 16** *Source:* https://en.wikipedia.org/w/index.php?title=File:US_Flag_raised_over_Shuri_castle_on_Okinawa.jpg *License:* Public Domain *Contributors:* User:W.wolny .................................................................................19

**Figure 17** *Source:* https://en.wikipedia.org/w/index.php?title=File:OkinawaJapanesePOW.jpg *License:* Public Domain *Contributors:* Al Silonov, Bohème, BotMultichill, BotMultichillT, Cla68, Falkmart, Kugel~commonswiki, Manxruler, Movieevery ..........................20

**Figure 18** *Source:* https://en.wikipedia.org *Contributors:* Cobatfor, Jwh, Kugel~commonswiki .....................................22

**Figure 19** *Source:* https://en.wikipedia.org/w/index.php?title=File:Attack_on_bloody_ridge.jpg *License:* Public Domain *Contributors:* User:W.wolny .................................................................................23

**Figure 20** *Source:* https://en.wikipedia.org/w/index.php?title=File:Last_picture_of_LtGen._Buckner_at_Okinawa.jpg *License:* Public Domain *Contributors:* USMC .................................................................................25

**Figure 21** *Source:* https://en.wikipedia.org/w/index.php?title=File:Japanese_POWs,_Okinawa_cph.3c32796.jpg *License:* Public Domain *Contributors:* U.S. Marine Corps .....................................26

**Figure 22** *Source:* https://en.wikipedia.org/w/index.php?title=File:Marine-observation-plane-okinawa.gif *License:* Public Domain *Contributors:* photographer: Lt. David D. Duncan, USMC .................................................27

**Figure 23** *Source:* https://en.wikipedia.org/w/index.php?title=File:OkinawaMarineOrphan.jpg *License:* Public Domain *Contributors:* Cla68, Fg2, Hohum, Kugel~commonswiki, Ruff tuff cream puff, 2 anonymous edits .....................................27

**Figure 24** *Source:* https://en.wikipedia.org/w/index.php?title=File:Overcoming_the_last_resistance.jpg *License:* Public Domain *Contributors:* User:W.wolny .................................................................................28

**Figure 25** *Source:* https://en.wikipedia.org/w/index.php?title=File:Kenneth_Glueck_USMC-110629-M-IV598-032.jpg *License:* Public Domain *Contributors:* Fæ, LittleWink, Maliepa, Reguyla, Tokorokoko .....................................31

**Figure 26** *Source:* https://en.wikipedia.org/w/index.php?title=File:V-J_Day_Celebration,_Okinawa,_August_1945_(15900085425).jpg *License:* Creative Commons Attribution 2.0 *Contributors:* USMC Archives from Quantico, USA .....................................31

**Image** *Source:* https://en.wikipedia.org/w/index.php?title=File:PD-icon.svg *License:* Public Domain *Contributors:* Alex.muller, Anomie, Anonymous Dissident, CBM, Jo-Jo Eumerus, MBisanz, PBS, Quadell, Rocket000, Strangerer, Timotheus Canens, 1 anonymous edits .....33

**Image** *Source:* https://en.wikipedia.org/w/index.php?title=File:Commons-logo.svg *License:* logo *Contributors:* Anomie, Callanecc, CambridgeBayWeather, Jo-Jo Eumerus, RHaworth .....................................34

**Image** *Source:* https://en.wikipedia.org/w/index.php?title=File:Battleship_Yamato_under_air_attack_April_1945.jpg *License:* Public Domain *Contributors:* BrokenSphere, Denniss, Flamarande~commonswiki, Get It, Makthorpe, O484, Pibwl, Rcbutcher, Rsteen, Schimmelreiter, Shizhao, 1 anonymous edits ..............................................................................37

**Image** *Source:* https://en.wikipedia.org/w/index.php?title=File:US_Naval_Jack_48_stars.svg *License:* Public Domain *Contributors:* User:Dual Freq 37

**Figure 27** *Source:* https://en.wikipedia.org/w/index.php?title=File:Ten-goMap1.png *License:* GNU Free Documentation License *Contributors:* en:User:Cla68 ..............................................................................40

# License

# Index

61

Seaplane, 46
Second World War, 23
Seiichi Itō, 2, 12, 37, 39
Seppuku, 21
Shinjitai, 38
Shinyō-class suicide motorboat, 12
Shore battery, 39
Shuri Castle, 19, 20
Signal flag, 45
Simon Bolivar Buckner Jr., 23
Simon Bolivar Buckner, Jr., 2, 5, 25
Solomon Islands campaign, 38
Sortie, 41
South Korea, 22
Soviet invasion of Manchuria, 32
Standard-type battleship, 41
Starboard, 44
Stars and Stripes (newspaper), 49
Starvation, 28
Stinson L-5 Sentinel, 27
Submarine, 12, 40
Suicide attack, 12
Supermarine Seafire, 11
Superstructure, 37, 43
Surface combatant, 38
Surrender of Japan, 47
Surveillance, 41

Taiwan, 22
Taiwan (island), 7, 13
Tameichi Hara, 48
Task Force 58, 37, 41
Tenth Army (United States), 5
Tenth United States Army, 2, 3
Teruto Tsubota, 29
The captain goes down with the ship, 45
The Guardian, 32
The Pinnacle, Battle of Okinawa, 16
The Rising Sun: The Decline and Fall of the
    Japanese Empire 1936–1945, 49
Thirty-Second Army (Japan), 2, 6
Thomas E. Watson (USMC), 5
Thompson submachine gun, 1
Tokuyama, Yamaguchi, 39
Torpedo, 37, 43
Torpedo bomber, 12, 41
Toyoda Soemu, 39

Underwater Demolition Team, 5
United Kingdom, 1, 22
United States, 1, 37, 38
United States Army, 3
United States Army Center of Military History,
    33

United States Civil Administration of the
    Ryukyu Islands, 32
United States Coast Guard, 22
United States Fifth Fleet, 2, 4, 11, 37, 41
United States Forces Japan, 33
United States Marine Corps, 3, 15
United States Third Fleet, 11
USS Alaska (CB-1), 42
USS Bataan (CVL-29), 41
USS Belleau Wood (CVL-24), 41
USS Bennett (DD-473), 47
USS Bennington (CV-20), 41
USS Bunker Hill (CV-17), 10, 41
USS Essex (CV-9), 41
USS Guam (CB-2), 42
USS Hackleback (SS-295), 40
USS Hancock (CV-19), 41
USS Hornet (CV-12), 41
USS Idaho (BB-42), 14
USS Indiana (BB-58), 41
USS Maryland (BB-46), 47
USS Massachusetts (BB-59), 41
USS Mississippi (BB-41), 21
USS Missouri (BB-63), 42
USS New Jersey (BB-62), 41
USS Panamint (AGC-13), 5
USS San Jacinto (CVL-30), 41
USS South Dakota (BB-57), 41
USS Threadfin (SS-410), 40
USS Wisconsin (BB-64), 42

Vice Admiral, 4
Victor Davis Hanson, 32
Victory in Europe Day, 17
Victory over Japan Day, 31
Vought F4U Corsair, 41, 42

Ward Wilson, 50
Wikipedia:Attribution needed, 29
Wikipedia:Citing sources, 32
Wikipedia:Please clarify, 11
William Halsey, 11
William Halsey, Jr., 2
William H. P. Blandy, 4
Withdrawal (military), 41
With the Old Breed: At Peleliu and Okinawa,
    34
World War I, 20
World War II, 1, 3, 37, 38

XXIV Corps (United States), 2, 5, 14

Yae-Dake, 15
Yomitan, Okinawa, 15, 39

62

www.ingramcontent.com/pod-product-compliance
Lightning Source LLC
Chambersburg PA
CBHW021144020426
42331CB00005B/891